PITCH
ANYTHING

PITCH
ANYTHING

An Innovative Method for
PRESENTING, PERSUADING,
AND WINNING THE DEAL

OREN KLAFF

New York   Chicago   San Francisco   Lisbon   London
Madrid   Mexico City   Milan   New Delhi   San Juan
Seoul   Singapore   Sydney   Toronto

19 20 QFR 21 20 19 18

ISBN: 978-0-07-175285-5
MHID: 0-07-175285-4

This publication is designed to provide accurate and authoritative information in regard to the subject matter covered. It is sold with the understanding that neither the author nor the publisher is engaged in rendering legal, accounting, or other professional service. If legal advice or other expert assistance is required, the services of a competent professional person should be sought.

—*From a Declaration of Principles Jointly Adopted by a Committee of the American Bar Association and a Committee of Publishers and Associations*

This work recounts real events. Some names and locations have been changed, at the request of the persons involved, to respect the nature of private financial transactions.

McGraw-Hill books are available at special quantity discounts to use as premiums and sales promotions, or for use in corporate training programs. To contact a representative, please visit the Contact Us pages at www.mhprofessional.com.

For Dad, true north

Contents

Chapter 1 The Method 1

Chapter 2 Frame Control 19

Chapter 3 Status 69

Chapter 4 Pitching Your Big Idea 95

Chapter 5 Frame Stacking and Hot Cognitions 129

Chapter 6 Eradicating Neediness 157

Chapter 7 Case Study: The Airport Deal 171

Chapter 8 Get in the Game 207

Index 219

PITCH
ANYTHING

Chapter 1

The Method

Here's the "big idea" in 76 words: There is a fundamental disconnect between the way we pitch anything and the way it is received by our audience. As a result, at the crucial moment, when it is most important to be convincing, nine out of ten times we are not. Our most important messages have a surprisingly low chance of getting through.

You need to understand why this disconnect occurs in order to overcome it, succeed, and profit. This book tells you how.

I Am Not a Natural

I pitch deals for a living. My job is to raise capital for businesses looking to expand rapidly or go public. I am good at it. When companies need money, I get it for them. I have raised millions for deals involving Marriott, Hershey's, Citigroup, and many other household names—and I continue to do so at a rate of about $2 million per week. From the outside, the reasons for my success seem simple: I offer wealthy investors profitable deals that involve Wall Street banks. But others do that, too. Yet I raise a lot more money than they do. They compete in the same market. Do the same types of deals. Pitch the same kinds of facts and figures. But the numbers show I am consistently one of the best. The difference isn't luck. It is not a special gift. And I have no background in sales. What I do have is a good method.

As it turns out, pitching is one of those business skills that depends heavily on the method you use and not how hard you try. Better method, more money. Much better method, much more money. It's no different for you. The better you are at advocating your position, the more successful you will be. Maybe you want to sell an idea to investors, convince a client to choose you over the other guy, or even explain to your boss why you should be paid more. I can help you get better at it using the five methods in this book.

Pitching a Master of the Universe

Over the years, I've pitched to—and closed deals with—some of the iconic businesspeople of our time, including founding members of Yahoo!, Google, and Qualcomm. But the story of what I can offer you cannot really be told without my explaining the day I went to pitch one of the guys Tom Wolfe would describe as a "master of the universe."

"Jonathan" (never Johnny or even John) is an investment banker who controls vast sums of capital. He gets between 600 and 800 pitches a year; that's three to four every business day. He often makes multimillion-dollar investment decisions based on no more information than a few e-mails on his BlackBerry.

As a dealmaker, this guy—and I have absolutely no intention of giving you his name; he sues everyone and anyone at a moment's notice—is the real deal.

There are three things you must know about Jonathan. First, he's a math phenom who can calculate yield curves in his head. He doesn't need spreadsheets. He can instantly analyze what you are pitching him. Second, he's seen more than 10,000 deals and can detect any kind of flaw or BS no matter how well hidden. Third, he's tough talking and, at the same time, witty and charismatic. The upshot: When he's pitching you, *his* chances are good. When you're pitching him, *yours* aren't. Yet, if you want to be taken seriously in venture capital, you need to have done a deal with this guy. And so, some years ago, when I was working to raise money for a software company, I arranged to pitch Jonathan and his investment team. Given their reputation, I knew if I got them on board, it would be a lot easier to raise money from other investors who were still undecided. They'd say, "Hey, if Jonathan signed off on this, then I'm in too." But Jonathan knew the power of his endorsement—and he wasn't going to give me an easy win.

As my pitch got underway, he made things difficult. Maybe it was for sport. Maybe he was having a bad day. But it was clear he wanted to take—and keep—control of the whole presentation. I didn't realize this at the start, however, so, I began, as I always do, by *framing* (frames create context and relevance; as we will see, the person who owns the frame owns the conversation). I explained exactly what I would—and would not—be talking about, and Jonathan immediately started giving me a type of resistance called *deframing*, which is exactly like it sounds.

For example, when I said, "We expect revenues to be $10 million next year," he cut me off and changed the frame with, "Who cares about your made-up revenue projections. Tell me what your *expenses* are going to be."

A minute later, I was explaining, "Our secret sauce is such-and-such advanced technology."

And he said, "No, that's not a secret sauce. That's just ketchup."

I knew not to react to these comments. I pressed on.

"We have a Fortune 50 company as our largest customer."

He interrupted with, "Look, I'm done here in nine minutes, so can you get to the point?"

He was really making it difficult. You can imagine how hard it was to use all the right techniques: *setting the frame, telling the story, revealing the intrigue, offering the prize, nailing the hookpoint, and getting the deal.*

Collectively, I call these the *STRONG method* (you will learn about these soon).

Some 12 minutes after I began, what I had hoped was going to be my best pitch ever instead showed all the signs of being my one of my worst.

Put yourself in my situation. After just 12 minutes of your presentation, you've been told that your secret sauce is ketchup. Told that your projections are made-up numbers. And that you have nine minutes left to actually make a point.

I was faced with the *presenter's problem:* You can have incredible knowledge about your subject. You can make your most important points clearly, even with passion, and you can be very well organized. You can do all those things as well as they can be done—and still not be convincing. That's because a great pitch is not about procedure. It's about getting and keeping attention. And that means you have to own the room with *frame control,* drive emotions with *intrigue pings,* and get to a *hookpoint* fairly quickly. (Details on those last two in a second.)

I reminded myself of these steps in the face of Jonathan's interruptions. Then I swallowed hard and hoped my nervousness wasn't showing. I went back to my pitch, concentrating on my three objectives. I was determined. When he deframed, I reframed. When he looked disinterested, I delivered an *intrigue ping* (this is a short but provocative piece of information that arouses curiosity): "By the way, an NFL quarterback is also an investor." And finally, I got him to the *hookpoint*, the place in the presentation where your listeners become emotionally engaged. Instead of you giving them information, they are asking you for more on their own. At the hookpoint, they go beyond interested to being involved and then committed.

At the end of the 21 minutes, my pitch was complete. I knew Jonathan was *in*. He leaned forward and whispered, "Forget the deal for a moment. What in the hell was that? Nobody pitches like that but *me*."

I tried to show no emotion as I told him, "*That*, in general terms, is called *neurofinance*, an idea that combines neuroscience—how the brain works—with economics. I have taken it a step further and have broken it down into five parts" (the method we talked about above).

Now, even though Jonathan has MENSA-level intelligence, he doesn't have much interest in concepts like neuroscience. He—maybe like you—had always believed that the ability to pitch was a natural talent. But given what he had just seen me do in 21 minutes—it changed his mind. It was clear my pitching was a learned skill and not naked, natural talent like his.

"You can do that all the time?" he asked.

"Yes," I said. "It's based on research about how the brain receives new ideas. And I'm raising a lot of money with it."

Jonathan hears a lot of big claims. When you listen to three or four pitches a day, your "BS detector" becomes finely tuned. So he asked, "How many hours do you have working on this neuro-whatever-it's-called?"

He was sure my answer was going to be 20 hours. Maybe 50. I shocked him when I said, "Over 10,000 hours."

He looked at me with a wry half-smile. Giving up all pretense of being disinterested, he said, "I need you on my team. Come do this for my deals, and you'll make a lot of money."

I had never been more flattered. Not only had Jonathan, a guy who had been on magazine covers, offered me a partnership, he had given me an even higher compliment—validation that my method worked in high-stakes situations.

I turned him down. He had a reputation for being difficult to work for, and no amount of money is worth that. But his reaction persuaded me to try my approach as part of an investment company. I joined Geyser Holdings in Beverly Hills, the most profitable venture firm you have never heard of. Even as the economy cooled down (and then frosted over), I helped take Geyser from $100 million to $400 million in about four years. How I did that can serve as your blueprint for success. As you will see, it's possible to use the PITCH method in any presentation where you need to be truly convincing. What worked for me will work for you—no matter what you do for a living.

The Need for a New Method

If ever there is a time to learn to pitch effectively, it is now. Funding is tight. Competition is more aggressive. On a good day, your customers are distracted by text messages, e-mails, and phone calls, and on a bad day, they are impossible to reach. If you've been in business for more than 10 minutes, you have figured this much out: The better you are at keeping someone's attention, the more likely that person will be to go for your idea.

But what kind of advice is this really? Telling someone, "Keep the audience's attention" is like telling someone learning to play tennis to "hit the ball with topspin when it comes." *They know that*! What they don't know is how to do it. But it's worth figuring out. If you have to sell anything as part of your job—a product, a service, an idea, and we all do at some point—you know how the right pitch can make a project go forward and the wrong pitch can kill it. You also understand how difficult it can be to pitch to a skeptical audience that is paying attention to you one minute and distracted by a phone call the next. But we all have to go through this because we all have to pitch if we need something. And though most of us spend less than 1 percent of our time doing it, pitching may be the most important thing we do. When we have to raise money, or sell a complicated idea, or get a promotion, we have to do it. And yet we do it incredibly badly.

One reason is that we are our own worst coach. We know way too much about our own subject to be able to understand how another person will experience it in our pitch, so we tend to overwhelm that person. (We will deal with this in Chapter 4.) But the biggest reason we fail is not our fault. As you will see in the pages that follow, we don't pitch well because there is an evolutionary flaw in our brain—a wiring kluge in our hardware—that we must understand and learn to deal with if we are ever going to pitch successfully.

Dealing with the Crocodile Brain

A brief history of how the brain developed will show

1. How the kluge got there.

2. Why pitching is so much more complicated than we first thought.

3. Why, as with any high-order skill, such as physics, mathematics, or medicine, pitching must be learned.

The three basic parts of the brain are shown in Figure 1.1.

First, the history. Recent breakthroughs in neuroscience show that our brain developed in three separate stages. First came the old brain, or "crocodile brain"—we'll call it the "croc brain" for short. It's responsible for the initial filtering of all incoming messages, it generates most survival fight-or-flight responses, and it produces strong, basic emotions, too. But when it comes to decision making, the croc brain's reasoning power is . . . well, primitive. It simply doesn't have a lot of capacity, and most of what it does have is devoted primarily to the things it takes to keep us alive. When I am referring to the croc brain, I am referring to this level.

The midbrain, which came next, determines the meaning of things and social situations. And finally, the neocortex evolved with a problem-solving ability and is able to think about complex issues and produce answers using reason.

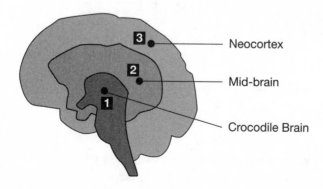

Figure 1.1 Three parts of the brain.

The Disconnect Between Message and Receiver

I learned from molecular biologist Craig Smucker that when we pitch something—an idea, product, deal, or whatever—the highest level of our brain, the neocortex, is doing the work. It's the neocortex that is forming ideas, putting them into language, and presenting them. This is fairly intuitive.

Three Brains Working Independently and Together

You can actually sense how the three parts of your brain work separately from each other.

When you are walking to your car and are surprised by someone shouting, you will first act reflexively with some fear. (This is the old crocodile/survival brain at work.)

Then, you will try to make meaning from the situation by identifying the person doing the yelling and placing him or her in a social context. This is your midbrain trying to determine if it is a friendly coworker, an angry parking attendant, or something worse.

Finally, you will process the situation in the neocortex, the problem-solving brain (which figures it out: "It's okay. It's just some guy yelling out to his buddy across the street.")

Our thought process exactly matches our evolution: First, survival. Then, social relationships. Finally, problem solving.

Pitching anything means explaining abstract concepts—so it didn't surprise me that ideas would be formed by the most modern, problem-solving part of the brain.

But this is exactly where my thinking—and probably yours— went off track. I assumed that if my idea-making abilities were

*located in the neocortex (as they are), then that's where the people
listening to my pitch were processing what I had to say.*

It's not.

Messages that are composed and sent by your young neocortex are received and processed by the other person's old crocodile brain.

You may be where I was about 10 years ago. Back then, I subscribed to "the brain is like a computer" metaphor. With a computer, if I send you an Excel spreadsheet file, you open it and read it in Excel. This is how I thought the brain worked. If I created a message in *my* smart neocortex and "sent" it over to you (by telling you about it), I figured that you'd be opening that message in *your* neocortex.

But no pitch or message is going to get to the logic center of the other person's brain without passing through the survival filters of the crocodile brain system first. And because of the way we evolved, those filters make pitching anything extremely difficult.

So instead of communicating with people, my best ideas were bouncing off their croc brains and crashing back into my face in the form of objections, disruptive behaviors, and lack of interest.

Ultimately, if they are successful, your pitches *do* work their way up to their neocortex eventually. And certainly by the time the other person is ready to say "Yes, we have a deal," he is dealing with the information at the highest logic center of his brain. But that is not where the other person initially hears what you have to say.

Let me explain further. Because we are a soft, weak, slow species compared with just about everything else out there, we survived for millions of years by viewing everything in the universe as potentially dangerous. And because very few situations we faced back then were safe, we learned to err on the side of extreme caution. And that continues (unconsciously) to this day every time we encounter something new. It happens whenever we encounter a pitch from someone who wants us to do something.

We are hardwired to be bad at pitching. It is caused by the way our brains have evolved.

The fact that you are pitching your idea from the neocortex but it is being received by the other person's croc brain is a serious problem.

It's the kluge we talked about earlier. The gap between the lower and upper brain is not measured in the two inches that separate them physically. It must be measured in millions of years (the five million years or so that it took for the neocortex to evolve, to be more precise). Why? Because while you are talking about "profit potential," "project synergy," "return on investment," and "why we should move forward now"—concepts your upper brain is comfortable with—the brain of the person on the other side of the desk isn't reacting to any of those highly evolved, relatively complicated ideas. It is reacting exactly as it should. It is trying to determine whether the information coming in is a threat to the person's immediate survival and, if it isn't, whether it can be ignored without consequence.

The Croc Brain at Work

As you are pitching your idea, the croc brain of the person sitting across from you isn't "listening" and thinking, "Hmmm, is this a good deal or not?" Its reaction to your pitch basically goes like this: "Since this is not an emergency, how can I ignore this or spend the least amount of time possible on it?"

This filtering system of the crocodile brain has a very short-sighted view of the world. Anything that is not a crisis it tries to mark as "spam."

If you got a chance to look at the croc brain's filtering instructions, it would look something like this:

1. If it's not dangerous, ignore it.
2. If it's not new and exciting, ignore it.
3. If it is new, summarize it as quickly as possible—and forget about the details.
   And finally there is this specific instruction:
4. *Do not* send anything up to the neocortex for problem solving unless you have a situation that is really unexpected and out of the ordinary.

These are the basic operating policies and procedures of our brains. No wonder pitching is so difficult.

Sure, after initial filtering, parts of your message move quickly through the midbrain and on to the neocortex—business meetings would be very odd otherwise—but the damage to your message and your pitch has already been done.

First, given the limited focus and capacity of the croc brain, up to 90 percent of your message is discarded before it's passed on up to the midbrain and then on to the neocortex. The crocodile brain just doesn't process details well, and it only passes along big, obvious chunks of concrete data.

Second, unless your message is presented in such a way that the crocodile brain views it to be new and exciting—*it is going to be ignored.*

Third, if your pitch is complicated—if it contains abstract language and lacks visual cues—then it is perceived as a threat. Not a threat in the sense that the person listening to your pitch fears he is going to be attacked, but a threat because without cues and context, the croc brain concludes that your pitch has the potential to absorb massive amounts of brain power to comprehend. And that is a major threat because there just isn't enough brain power to handle survival needs, the problems of day-to-day life, and existing work problems plus whatever unclear thing you are asking it to do. Presented with this kind of situation, a circuit breaker in your brain is tripped. The result? A neurotoxin gets attached to the potentially threatening message (your pitch). This is like a FedEx tracking number, which, in turn, routes your message to the amygdala for processing—and destruction.

Now, if there is one place in the brain you do not want your pitch to end up, it is the amygdala. This is the fear circuitry of the brain. The amygdala turns messages into physical sensations like a faster heart rate, sweating, increased breathing, and increased anxiety. And it produces a feeling that makes the person want to escape from the presentation.

Pitches are sent from the modern—and smart—part of the brain: the neocortex. But they are received by a part of the brain that is 5 million years older (and not as bright.)

This is a serious problem if you are trying to pitch anything.

Again, this is part of the hardwiring that has allowed us to survive. A lion is chasing you, and without needing to kick it up to your highly evolved neocortex (which would spend a lot of time trying to solve the problem), the *danger* switch in the amygdala is flipped *on*, and it sends the alarm to the rest of the brain to start spitting out chemical and electrical messages that get you to *Run!* before you even have a chance to think. And while we don't live in the wild any longer, our brains are still wired to work this way.

Everything in the recent research points to the same conclusion: Nine out of 10 messages that enter the crocodile brain—and remember, every single pitch starts by going through the crocodile brain—end up being coded.

- Boring: Ignore it.
- Dangerous: Fight/run.
- Complicated: Radically summarize (invariably causing a lot to be lost in the process) and pass it in severely truncated form.

We've been thinking about this all wrong for years. Clearly, we need a new way of pitching.

Rules of Engagement

There are the two questions we always ask ourselves after we have made a presentation or pitch:

1. Did I get through?
2. Was my message well received?

We assume that our audience will do what we want them to do if our idea is good, if we didn't stumble through the pitch, and if we showed a winning personality. Turns out, it doesn't work that way. What is vitally important is making sure your message fulfills two objectives: First, you don't want your message to trigger fear alarms. And second, you want to make sure it gets recognized as something positive, unexpected, and out of the ordinary—a pleasant novelty.

Bypassing those fear alarm sensors can be extremely difficult. Creating novelty in the message can be tricky, too. But it is the only way our pitch stands any chance whatsoever because the crocodile brain wants information a certain way—simple, clear, nonthreatening, and above all, intriguing and novel. You need to communicate in these ways, or you are never going to capture people's attention.

> The croc brain is picky and a cognitive miser whose primary interest is survival. It doesn't like to do a lot of work and is high maintenance when it is forced to perform. It requires concrete evidence—presented simply in black and white—to make a decision. Minor points of differentiation don't interest it. And this is the brain to which you are pitching.

As the principal gateway to the mind, the croc brain doesn't have a lot of time to devote to new projects. It's overseeing a big, complex operation (taking care of survival) and can't get bogged down in nuance and details. It likes facts clearly explained. It wants to choose between just two clearly explained options. And it needs you to get to the point fast. It goes to sleep during PowerPoint presentations, and it needs strong summarizing points to keep its attention.

If it gets really excited about some new project you have presented, then it approves it. Otherwise, it gives up on it, doesn't give it another thought, and goes on to the next issue.

The harsh but true reality is that the croc brain—the source of your target's first reaction to your pitch—is

- Going to ignore you if possible.
- Only focused on the big picture (and needs high-contrast and well-differentiated options to choose between).

- Emotional, in the sense it will respond emotionally to what it sees and hears, but most of the time that emotional response is fear.

- Focused on the here and now with a short attention span that craves novelty.

- In need of concrete facts—it looks for verified evidence and doesn't like abstract concepts.

When I learned these rules of engagement for dealing with the crocodile brain, I had my big "Aha" moment. I understood two very important things: First, I finally *got* the fundamental problem you and I have when we pitch something: We have our highly evolved neocortex, which is full of details and abstract concepts, trying to persuade the crocodile brain, which is afraid of almost everything and needs very simple, clear, direct, and nonthreatening ideas to decide in our favor. Second, I realized that when my pitches had gone well, I had inadvertently adhered to the five rules of engagement contained in the bullet points above. I had made the crocodile brain feel safe; I was feeding it short vignettes of clear, visual, and novel information; and I wasn't making it do much work. (I also understood that when I didn't stick to those rules of engagement, I usually failed.)

Why do these rules of engagement matter for pitching? Sometimes they don't. If you're pitching the Google Android phone, 3D television, or a Ferrari coupe, the brain becomes so flooded with dopamine—a chemical in your brain that sends messages about pleasure and rewards—that any old pitch will work. But short of having a product that's so sexy it's irresistible—you have to observe the rules about how the brain works. How to do this makes up the heart of this book.

What Comes Next

What became clear to me after my big "Aha" moment was that I needed to bridge the gap between the way the neocortex and crocodile brain see the world. More specifically, if I wanted my pitch to get through, I needed to be able to translate all the complex ideas coming out of my neocortex and present them in a way that the crocodile brain of the person I was pitching could easily accept and pay attention to.

It took me countless efforts to come up with a formula that worked. Now you are going to learn that formula.

As you will see, it begins by *setting the frame* for your pitch, putting your big idea into an easily understood context. And then, once the frame is established, you must seize *high social status* so that you have a solid platform from which to pitch. Then you must create messages that are full of *intrigue* and *novelty*.

To make this process easier to remember, I use the acronym *STRONG*:

Set the frame
Tell the story
Reveal the intrigue
Offer the prize
Nail the hookpoint
Get the deal

Over the years, I've used this formula—which we will be exploring in detail—in deal after deal with executives from Bear Stearns, Boeing, Disney, Honda, LinkedIn, Texas Instruments, and Yamaha. Each time I pitched, I learned more about the behaviors of the croc brain, and I eventually came to the understanding that there are five separate places where you can stumble in a pitch. Each step in the process represents one of these points where missteps can be fatal. When the other person's croc brain becomes either bored, confused, or threatened, your pitch is in trouble.

In the pages ahead I will discuss how to avoid those problems and create the perfect pitch, one that gains the full endorsement of the croc brain and increases your chances of success dramatically.

Chapter 2

Frame Control

It was July 2001, and I stood in front of a towering office in the heart of Beverly Hills. This was a corridor of power, both in Hollywood and the financial world, a place where careers were made, a place where deals got done.

And here I was, headed to the office of a guy who controlled close to $1 billion in assets. It's not every day you pitch someone with this level of influence. If you think I was nervous, think again. For once, I wasn't pitching. Instead, a colleague, Tom Davis, would be pitching to this icon of corporate finance, Bill Belzberg, one of the three billionaire Belzberg brothers.

You might have heard of the Belzbergs if you follow the business press. They rose to prominence as corporate raiders in the 1980s. Merely observing one of them in the boardroom was a master class in finance, so I was looking forward to what would materialize in the next hour.

Tom was 31, charismatic, a likeable CEO type. He had a nice company in place, but he lacked the money to grow. To get that money, he was willing to try the impossible—impress Belzberg.

I smiled to myself. This was going to be interesting. I'd watched Tom rehearse his presentation, and he had good instincts.

"My pitch is totally bulletproof, I have nerves of steel, and I'm bringing my A-game," he had said while we were waiting in Belzberg's lobby. His confidence was inspiring.

"We'll see," I said. "Just relax."

Soon after that, we were moved to the conference room. After more than 30 minutes of waiting, we watched as the double doors swung open. Bill Belzberg strode through as if entering a saloon. At 69 years old, he was tall and lanky. He waved his arm at Tom, motioning him to get started. Tom looked at me, and I nodded the go-ahead. Belzberg remained standing and almost immediately cut Tom off, "Look, I only want to know two things from you. What are monthly expenses, and how much are you paying yourself?"

Not what Tom wanted to hear. He had a different pitch planned, and now he was looking foolish, searching his bag to find expense charts. Where were the confidence and nerves of hardened titanium? He dropped his papers and stuttered a bit. He was lost.

Belzberg had said only 20 words. As you will see, it's possible for a 20-word disruption to control the fate of any deal. Why is that? An analogy, like the one below, might help explain all this.

Imagine for a moment that there is some kind of powerful energy field that surrounds all of us, silently transmitting from the depths of our subconscious. This invisible defense shield is genetically designed to protect our conscious minds from sudden intrusion by ideas and perspectives that are not our own.

When that energy field is overwhelmed, however, it collapses. Our mental defenses fail, and we become subject to another person's ideas, desires, and commands. That person can impose his will.

No one really knows whether there are human energy fields or not, but perhaps this is the best way to think about the mental structures that shape the way we see the world, which I call *frames*. And in a moment, you will begin to understand what happened when Tom's frame came into contact with—and collapsed under—Bill Belzberg's power frame.

Imagine looking at the world through a window frame that you hold in your hands. As you move the frame around, the sounds and images you encounter are interpreted by your brain in ways that are consistent with your intelligence, values, and ethics. This is your *point of view*.

Another person can look at the same thing through his own frame, and what he hears and sees may differ—by a little or a lot.

The common label given to this is *perspective*. I might perceive and interpret things differently than you do—which is a good thing. Another perspective is often what we need as we nurture our ideas and values.

Yet, as we interpret the world through our frames, something else happens. Our brains process what our senses tell us and quickly react with a series of questions: Is it dangerous? Should I eat it or mate with it? This is the croc brain at work, doing what it does best—detecting frames, protecting us from threats, and using dominance and aggression to deflect attacking ideas and information.

There are millions of people in the business world, and each brings a frame to his or her social encounters. Whenever two or more people come together to communicate in a business setting, their frames square off and then come into contact, but not in a cooperative or friendly manner. Frames are extremely competitive—remember, they are rooted in our survival instincts—and they seek to sustain dominance.

When frames come together, the first thing they do is collide. And this isn't a friendly competition—it's a *death match*. Frames don't merge. They don't blend. And they don't intermingle. *They collide, and the stronger frame absorbs the weaker.*

Only one frame will dominate after the exchange, and the other frames will be subordinate to the winner. *This is what happens below the surface of every business meeting you attend, every sales call you make, and every person-to-person business communication you have.*

The moment your frame makes contact with the frame of the person you are calling on, they clash, battle, and grapple for dominance. If your frame wins, you will enjoy *frame control*, where your ideas are accepted (and followed) by the others. But if your frame loses, though, you will be at the mercy of your customer, and your success will depend on that customer's charity.

Understanding how to harness and apply the power of frames is the most important thing you will ever learn.

Frame-Based Business

One of the many benefits of using a frame-based approach to doing business is that it does not require a lot of technique, tactics, or smooth talk. In fact, as you will soon see, the less you say, the more effective you will be.

Sales techniques were created for people who have already lost the frame collision and are struggling to do business from a subordinated or low-status position. The sad fact is, these methods are typically ineffective and usually end up offending people instead of promoting pleasant, mutually beneficial business.

For decades, there have been many books and seminars—there are more than 35,000 on Amazon—promoting methods to persuade, influence, cajole, and browbeat customers into making rapid purchase decisions. Many years ago, when the promoters of these programs realized how inefficient their methods were, they explained it away with the *law of large numbers*. Their typical promise is "Make 100 sales calls using our sales technique, and you will land two sales." In other words, work much, much harder than everyone else, and you will get a 2 percent success rate. But really, *what kind of success is that*?

What these sales gurus are missing is this: When you fail to control the *social frame*, you probably have already lost. All you can do then is fight for survival by fast talking, spin selling, trial closing, and a myriad of equally ineffective and annoying tactics that signal to the customer that you are needy and desperate—and defeated.

By preaching the law of large numbers, the purveyors of sales techniques are asking you to work longer and harder, with no real competitive advantage. They are forcing you to compensate for your weak position with a Herculean effort to win new business, claiming that *it's just a numbers game*. It's rather rude of them to give away so much of your life this way, isn't it?

Frame-based business takes the opposite approach. It promotes the use of social dynamics, stacking things in your favor before the game even begins.

When we think back about why this pitch or that pitch failed, we usually arrive at the fact that the terms of the deal weren't right for the buyer. Or we had a bad day and didn't position things correctly. Or the potential buyer found something he or she liked better. The reality is, however, that a pitch will fail for reasons that are far less obvious. And that's because frame control is won or lost even before the pitch starts.

When you own the frame, you are positioned to reach an agreement with your buyer. And you are also in a position to decide which deals, orders, or projects you want to work on instead of taking what you can get.

Think it's not possible? I do it every day and for the simple reason that I want to serve my buyers well. I can't do that if I'm continuously engaged in a frantic chase for new business.

Instead of flogging yourself to the point of exhaustion by making dozens of mind-numbingly unproductive sales calls and presentations, I'm going to show you how to get, and keep, frame control. And you are more likely to find yourself pitching five deals, tossing out the two deals you don't like, and keeping the three that interest you. How do you like my law of large numbers? This is what I do and what I have been doing for years.

Own the Frame, Win the Game

Let's do a quick review: A frame is the instrument you use to package your power, authority, strength, information, and status.

1. Everyone uses frames whether they realize it or not.
2. Every social encounter brings different frames together.
3. Frames do not coexist in the same time and place for long. They crash into each other, and one or the other gains control.
4. Only one frame survives. The others break and are absorbed. Stronger frames always absorb weaker frames.

5. The winning frame governs the social interaction. It is said to have frame control.

The Cop Frame: An Introduction to How Frames Work

So that you can become familiar with the terminology of frames and the basic function of frames in social encounters, here is an example of a dominant frame that you already know about—an almost textbook example of frame control.

Imagine you are driving along California's Highway 101 north of Santa Cruz. The weather and the scenery are intoxicating, as is the rush of speed you feel as you take the fast lane at 80 mph in your pursuit of the setting sun. The moment is perfect—until you see those flashing lights in your rearview mirror. It's a police interceptor. The *whoop-whoop* from a piercing siren and the Technicolor strobing of the light bar alert your croc brain that danger is imminent. *Dammit, where did he come from? How fast was I going?* These are the last few thoughts going through your neocortex before fear (a basic and primal emotion) sets in, and your croc brain seizes control of your actions. You are now "pulled over." As you reach for your license and registration, you see the cop approaching in the driver-side mirror.

As you will see from this example, frames make human communication simple because they package a particular perspective and all the information that goes with it.

You roll down the window. In this moment, two frames are about to collide: the cop's frame and yours.

Quick! What is your frame made of? "I was going with the flow of traffic" or "I thought the speed limit was higher out this way."

You settle on the "nice guy" frame: "Officer, I'm usually a good driver. How about cutting me a break this one time?"

But the cop frame is nearly invincible. It's reinforced—morally, socially, and politically. Oh yeah, he's got you on a speed gun, too.

You meekly smile as you hand him your license and registration. He pauses, scowling at you through his mirrored aviators. Now, your "nice guy" frame is about to be disrupted. "Do you know why I pulled you over?" he asks.

You know you were speeding. Because you do not have any higher moral authority to bring to the frame game, your frame will be destroyed. This is the key to frame control. *When you are responding ineffectively to things the other person is saying and doing, that person owns the frame, and you are being frame-controlled.*

Of course, there's no mystery about the outcome here. The officer has the stronger frame. Your two frames collided, and the cop frame won.

I chose this example so you could see how lesser frames literally crumble under a frame built from authority, status, and power. In this example, the officer had every form of power possible: physical, political, and moral power (you broke the law, and you knew it).

Let's explore the officer's frame on a deeper level so as to understand what really happened. The silhouette of his cruiser in your rearview mirror and the flashing lights pulled your primal levers of fear, anxiety, and obedience. Your croc brain went into defense mode. Your stomach tightened. Your breathing accelerated, along with your heart rate, and blood rushed to your face. All this happened the moment your croc brain was alarmed. You couldn't come up with any frame, any perspective, any way to view the situation that would be strong enough to break the officer's frame.

The lesson of the cop frame is an essential one: *If you have to explain your authority, power, position, leverage, and advantage, you do not hold the stronger frame.* Rational appeals to higher order, logical thinking never win frame collisions or gain frame control. Notice, the officer does not need to pitch you on why he is going to issue you a citation. He does not need to rationalize with you. He doesn't have to explain his power, he doesn't need to rest a hand on his gun, and he doesn't need to describe to you what will happen if you decide to resist. He feels no need to explain how critical it is that you remain calm and obedient. He doesn't suggest that you have fear and anxiety. Your croc brain instantly and naturally has these reactions to the cop frame. You are reacting; your croc brain is in control. Your actions are automatic, primal, and beyond your grasp.

In the final moments of the social encounter, the officer hands you the ticket. This roadside meeting is over. The only other thing he says to you is: "Sign here. Press hard. Fifth copy is yours."

Finally, not quite an afterthought but perhaps intended as a reward for your calm obedience, he says, "Slow down, and have a nice day," crowning your defeat with shame. *Every social interaction is a collision of frames, and the stronger frame always wins. Frame collisions are primal. They freeze out the neocortex and bring the crocodile brain in to make decisions and determine actions.*

Strong frames are impervious to rational arguments. Weak arguments, made up of logical discussions and facts, just bounce off strong frames.

Over the years, I observed that a successful pitch depends on your ability to build strong frames that are impervious to rational arguments. These strong frames can break weak frames and then absorb them. Is there a formula for creating such a frame and using it? Turns out, there is.

Choosing a Frame

Whenever you are entering a business situation, the first question you must ask is, "What kind of frame am I up against?" The answer will depend on several factors, including the relative importance of your offering to the business interests of your buyer. But know this: Frames mainly involve basic desires. These are the domain of the croc brain. It would be fair to say that strong frames *activate basic desires.*

One way to think about this is that there are only a few basic approaches that the buyer's croc brain reacts to, so you don't need to carefully *tune* each frame to individual personalities. If you were a mechanic reaching into your toolbox, then a frame would be more like a rubber mallet than a screwdriver.

I think of these things before I take a meeting: What are the basic primal attitudes and emotions that will be at play? Then I make simple decisions about the kind of frame I want to go in with. For many years, I used just four frames that would cover every business situation. For example, if I know the person I'm meeting is a hard-charging, type A personality, I will go in with a *power-busting frame.* If that person is an analytical, dollars-and-cents type, I will choose an *intrigue frame.* If I'm outnumbered and out-gunned and the deck is stacked against me, *time frames* and *prize frames* are essential.

I am also ready and willing to switch to a different frame as the social interaction develops or changes.

Going into most business situations, there are three major types of opposing frames that you will encounter:

1. Power frame
2. Time frame
3. Analyst frame

You have three major response frame types that you can use to meet these oncoming frames, win the initial collision, and control the agenda:

1. Power-busting frame
2. Time constraining frame
3. Intrigue frame
   There is a fourth frame you can deploy. It's useful against all three of the opposing frames and many others you will encounter:
4. Prize frame

What follows is a discussion of how you can recognize opposing frames and defeat them.

The Power Frame

The most common opposing frame you will encounter in a business setting is the *power frame*. The power frame comes from the individual who has a massive ego. His power is rooted in his status—a status derived from the fact that others give this person honor and respect. You will know that you are facing a power frame when you encounter arrogance, lack of interest (a vibe that conveys "I'm more important than you"), rudeness, and similar imperial behaviors.

Power frame types (a.k.a. big shots, egomaniacs—whatever you want to call them) tend to be oblivious to what others think. They are more likely to pursue the satisfaction of their own appetites. They are often poor judges of the reactions of others. They are more likely to hold stereotypes. They can be overly optimistic. And they are more likely to take unmeasured risks.

They are also the most vulnerable to your power-busting frame because they do not expect it. They expect your fawning deference and obedience. They expect you to laugh at their bad jokes. They expect you to value their feelings above your own. They expect you to adopt their frame. Therein lies their weakness. Not for a moment do they think that your frame is going to take control. You will almost always take them by surprise.

When you approach an opposing power frame, your first and most important objective is to avoid falling into the other person's frame by reacting to it. And make absolutely certain that you do nothing that strengthens the other person's frame before your frames collide.

Observing power rituals in business situations—such as acting deferential, engaging in meaningless small talk, or letting yourself be told what to do—reinforces the alpha status of your target and confirms your subordinate position. *Do not do this*!

As the opposing power frame approaches, when you first encounter the person you are meeting, you must be prepared for the frame collision to happen at any moment.

Prepare well and your frame will disrupt his, causing a momentary equilibrium in the social forces in the room, and then your frame will overtake and absorb his.

This all sounds like high drama, but in practice, it is often swift and tranquil. Before your target realizes what has occurred, control of the frame has shifted. Once you get used to establishing the dominant frame, it will become second nature. And when it does, you are going to have the time of your life.

Encountering the Power Frame

Several years ago, I had a meeting at a large money center bank whose name you would recognize in an instant. This was supposed to be a one-hour meeting, and it was made clear by the guy we were meeting that he would give us precisely *one* hour. This is classic power framing with hard time pressure thrown in.

The cost of getting our team to Washington for this pitch was more than $20,000. But the meeting could be worth millions if we pitched it right.

After my team and I were escorted through security, we rode the elevator to the nineteenth floor, where more than *$1 trillion* worth of business was traded each year. We felt like we were about to take a place among the nation's most powerful and elite financial traders.

Thirty-five traders moved billions of dollars a month here, and we were one hour away from being part of the game. I had contacted all my investors, and together we had pooled about $60 million in investment money that I was bringing to the table.

My contact, a trader named Steve, was meeting us, and I would be pitching him and two analysts. After a long wait, an impeccably dressed young woman led us to the largest conference room I've ever seen, about half the size of a basketball court. Steve and his entourage came in and exchanged the standard pleasantries. Steve was one of the bigger volume traders on the floor. He showed up several minutes late and then spent 15 minutes talking about himself. A precious 22 minutes had been burned. Finally, I was able to hand out our materials and begin the pitch.

During the economic boom of the time, Steve had become accustomed to doing $100 million deals that would close in a single day; by contrast, we had a $60 million deal that would take at least 30 days to close. So he didn't seem terribly interested.

I talked about the types of assets we wanted to buy and what we would pay. During a moment of pause, I looked over at Steve. He had taken our pitch book, flipped it over, and was absent-mindedly tracing his hand on the back of it with a pen.

How significant is this lack of attention? Well, it's pretty bad. However, if you view the world through the lens of traditional sales techniques, you would think there's something wrong with my information or my deal. But instead, if you view the world through frames and social dynamics, then you would understand that the *deal was fine.* This is just the power frame coming at you, and in the collision of frames, you've just lost.

I first thought, *Ouch, how could this be happening?* I had burned a lot of time and money getting to this meeting, and I could see our opportunity slipping away. The guy was *tracing his hand* on *my* executive summary. I felt two inches tall. My crocodile brain became overwhelmed with basic, primal emotions. I was frame-controlled. My simple, emotional, reactive croc brain told me to run, and I considered it.

When you abide by the rituals of power instead of establishing your own, you reinforce the opposing power frame.

I soon recovered my poise, and here is what followed:

"Steve, gimme that," I said, pulling the pitch book away
    from him.
That's a power frame disrupter.
Dramatic pause . . .

I looked at Steve's drawing intently. "Hold on, wait a sec. Now I see what's going on. This drawing is pretty damn good. Forget the big deal for a minute. How about you sell this to me. Name a price."

This is an extreme example of high-stakes power frames. But you can do this in everyday meetings in a far less dramatic way to change and refocus the frame to a totally different subject. If a guy is going to dominate you, let him dominate you on the price of something like a hand drawing in this case, something that doesn't matter. If you find yourself in a similar situation (the day will come when this happens to you, too), then pick something abstract and start an intense price negotiation over it—and it doesn't matter if you win or lose. The power of the person's frame is rendered trivial, and the focus is back to you and what you want to do with the meeting.

Steve didn't expect this, and the concussion from the force of my frame-busting move completely changed the dynamic of that moment and the remainder of the meeting. I got another chance to get the focus back on the real subject—the $60 million I was there to spend. And now I had Steve's complete attention.

To instigate a power frame collision, use a mildly shocking but not unfriendly act to cause it. Use defiance and light humor. This captures attention and elevates your status by creating something called "local star power." (You will read about creating status and local star power in Chapter 3.)

Taking the Frame

Here are some subtler examples of taking the power frame away. As soon as you come in contact with your target, look for the first opportunity to

1. Perpetrate a small denial, or
2. Act out some type of defiance.

Examples

You place a folder on the conference table that is labeled "Confidential—John Smith." When the target reaches for the file, you grab it and say, "Uh-uh, not yet. You have to wait for this."

If you deal in creative work and you brought visuals, let the target sneak a peek and then, when you see him curiously looking, turn it over, take it away, and deliver a soft reprimand that says, *not until I say you're ready*.

This is a quick tease followed by a strong denial, and it is massively disruptive to the target's croc brain. What you are doing is not offensive, and it's not mean. It's playful, and it tells the target subconsciously, "I'm the one in charge here, not you, my friend."

The key to taking the frame is to perpetrate the denial and make it clear: Not yet. This is my meeting, we're following my agenda, and everything that happens will be on my timeline.

Another way to control the frame is to respond to a comment with a small but forceful act of defiance.

TARGET: "Thanks for coming over. I only have 15 minutes this afternoon."

YOU: "That's okay, I only have 12." *You smile. But you are serious, too.*

With this simple remark, you have just snatched the power frame away from your target. This can easily become a frame game. I've had meetings get cut down to just two minutes this way. They will say, you only have 12 minutes? I forgot, I only have 10. Then I will come back with 8. And so on. As you'll find out, these kinds of frame games are good for relationships. They are a way of *prizing* (which you will read about next) and can be entertaining for both parties. It can be that simple. The better you are at giving and taking frame control, the more successful you will be.

Think of how many ways you can use small acts of denial and defiance in the opening moments of meetings. The possibilities are only limited by your imagination. Defiance and light humor are the keys to seizing power and frame control. Keep it fun, do it with a grin on your face, and the moment the power shifts to you, move the meeting forward in the direction you want. This is the foundation of frame control. You'll be seizing more power and status as the pitch continues.

Power shifts and frame grabs start small and escalate quickly. When this first power transfer takes place, when your target loses the frame, he knows it—he can feel that something just happened. His cognition is hot, which means that his basic desires have been activated. Now, he is paying close attention and is fully engaged. He is thinking, *Whoa, what do we have here?*

He might be feeling a little buzz from what you've just done but is not offended because you were not rude or mean. *When you are defiant and funny at the same time, he is pleasantly challenged by you and instinctively knows that he is in the presence of a pro.* This is the moment when he realizes that this is a game, that the game is now *on*, and that you are both about to have a lot of fun playing it.

Once started, the game has its own inertia, and you can use it to your advantage. Don't be afraid to play with your power by engaging in a little give and take to keep his attention in the moment because that is the entire purpose of this game—*to capture and keep attention until your pitch is complete.*

You must also take care not to abuse the power you now hold. The *frame master*, which is what you will be when you get good at this, knows that dominating the frame is not *how* you win the game but rather a *means* to win the game. No one likes to be dominated, so once you own the frame, use this power in ways that are fun and mutually exciting.

Small acts of denial and defiance are enormously powerful frame disrupters. They equalize the social power structure and then transfer all that power to you. Then, all you need to do is hold on to the power and use it wisely.

The Prize Frame

Another common situation occurs when the key decision maker does not attend the meeting as was agreed to. This situation requires a special kind of response that not only will reaffirm your control of the frame but also will establish you as someone unlike anyone else they have dealt with.

Let's say that you've done everything right so far. You've come into the business interaction and quickly asserted strong frames and, hopefully, frame control with the people you've just met. You're ready to start your pitch and are waiting for "Mr. Big" to come in, when his assistant steps in to announce, "I am so sorry. Mr. Big just called. He can't make the meeting for another hour. He says to start without him." She turns to leave.

This is a defining moment for you. You have just lost the frame, and there is nothing you can do about it. However, this does not mean that you do not have choices. Your options are

1. Go ahead with your presentation, even though you know you've lost the frame, hope for the best, and hope that maybe Mr. Big will join the group toward the end of the meeting. I would not recommend this.
2. *Stop everything.* Reframe using power, time, or prize frames (which are covered in this chapter) or perhaps all three. Immediately take the power back.

You've traveled to this meeting, prepared for it, and have an established goal. Are you willing to throw that away?

No one can tell your story as well as you can. If you trust your presentation to subordinates and expect them to pass it on to the decision maker with the same force and qualities of persuasion that you have, then you are not being honest with yourself. Again, no one can tell your story as well as you can. Mr. Big must hear it. *He must hear it from you.*

This is what I usually say in this situation:

"So you guys are asking me to delay the start? Okay. I can give you 15 minutes to get organized. But if we can't start by then, *then let's just call it a day.*"

Usually someone will volunteer to track down Mr. Big, and that person will try as hard as he or she can to find him and request that he join the meeting.

Or someone will say, "Let's go ahead with the presentation, and we'll make sure that Mr. Big is briefed." You can't let your frame get absorbed by this. Your response? "No, we're not going to follow your agenda. This meeting is going to start when I say *start*, and it will end when I say *stop*. You're going to make sure that all the right people come to the meeting on time. Then we're only going to cover the items on my agenda, and you're going pay attention to every minute of my presentation."

You only *think* this way, of course. What you actually say is, "I can wait 15 minutes, but then I have to leave." That's enough to get the message through.

The first time you think this way and say these words, you'll be uncomfortable—no, make that terrified—and you'll wonder if you are doing the right thing. Your heart will race, and you'll fear the consequences of your boldness, afraid of having offended your audience. You'll second-guess yourself and think you've just made an awful mistake.

And then something awesome will happen. The people in the room will scramble, doing their best to prevent you from being offended, doing their best to keep you from leaving. They are worried about *you*.

When you own the frame, others react to *you*.

Like Peter Parker's transformation into Spiderman, you will suddenly be empowered by an internal change state that is felt by everyone in the room. Be judicious with this power as you are now in complete control of the situation. If you stand, pack up your things, and leave, it will be a social disaster for Mr. Big and his staff. So be benevolent, give Mr. Big the promised 15 minutes to arrive, and act politely but true to your frame.

And if he does not show at that point, you leave. You do not deliver your presentation, you do not leave brochures, and you do not apologize. *Your* time has been wasted, and you don't even need to say it. They know.

If it seems appropriate, and if this is a company with which you want to do business, tell the most important person in the room that you are willing to reschedule—on your turf. That's right, you offer to reschedule and acknowledge that these things happen (we have all missed meetings before), but for the next meeting, they must come to you.

This is a subtle framing technique known as prizing. What you do is reframe everything your audience does and says as if they are trying to win you over.

A few moments earlier, you learned that Mr. Big wasn't coming to your meeting and apparently you were just the morning entertainment. Now, however, you are communicating to your buyers that *they are here to entertain you*. What prizing subconsciously says to your audience is, "You are trying to win my attention. I am the prize, not you. I can find a thousand buyers (audiences, investors, or clients) like you. There is only one me."

It also conveys to your audience that if they wish to get any further information from you, they will first have to do something to earn it.

Prizing 101

To solidify the prize frame, you make the buyer qualify himself to you. "Can you tell me more about yourself? I'm picky about who I work with." At a primal, croc brain level, you have just issued a challenge: *Why do I want to do business with you?*

This is a powerful and unspoken expression of your high status and your frame dominance. It forces your audience to qualify themselves by telling you exactly how interested they really are.

Sound outrageous? It's not, I promise you. *When you rotate the circle of social power 180 degrees, it changes everything.* The predator becomes the prey. In this instance, what your target is feeling is a kind of moral shame—they have wronged you—and they feel obligated to make things right.

Initially, you walked in with low status. Just another pitch in a long string of pitches. Over many experiences, these people have learned how to have their way with salespeople and presenters like you. But now, you've broken their power play. They will apologize, appease, and try to correct for the social gaffe, and in most cases, if Mr. Big is in the building, they will find a way to get him in front of you.

In a moment, I'm going to address what happens when you encounter *time frames* and *analyst frames*. Before going into these aspects of framing in greater detail, though, I think it might help to prepare the ground if I recount how I came to develop and use frames over the years. As you will see, the practical side of frames grew out of my personal experiences, sometimes in high-stakes situations where there was much to be gained and lost.

Remember, when you own the frame, people respond to you. Let me share an example from my own experience.

The Avocado Farmer's Money

I looked down at my phone. Fourteen missed calls, all from the same person, D. WALTER. I'd turned off my ringer for less than 30 minutes, and the phone blew up. I listened to one of his messages:

"Oren, I have a serious problem," he started.

His serious problem was a deal that had already gone bad, and now it was my job to help.

Dennis Walter was an avocado farmer, a guy who got his overalls dirty, a guy who put in long days in the hot sun. After 35 years, he was ready for retirement. He had money saved, but a good portion of it ($640,000) was in an escrow account, controlled by a man named Donald McGhan.

Dennis wanted his money now, and it was his, legally. But he was unable to get it back despite repeated attempts. This was now affecting an $18 million deal that both Dennis and I were in. If Dennis couldn't wire his money to me, all $640,000, then the deal—a large property we were buying in Hawaii—would start to unwind. So his problem was now my problem, too.

To retrieve Dennis's money, I would have to sit down with McGhan and make an appeal to have the money returned. This is how I was thrust into a pitch that clearly was doomed to fail. It wasn't life and death, but it was close. This was a man's life savings.

I knew a little bit about McGhan. He had a reputation as a successful businessman, primarily in the field of medical devices. Intriguingly, while at Dow Corning in the 1960s, he helped to invent the first generation of silicone breast implants. Today, he owned two companies: MediCor and Southwest Exchange.

MediCor's breast implant business had looked promising for a while. But the success enjoyed there was short-lived, and McGhan turned desperate. To keep MediCor solvent, McGhan began siphoning money from Southwest Exchange.

Southwest Exchange, which McGhan bought in 2004, gave him instant access to over $100 million in escrow accounts. Real estate investors, like Dennis, had used Southwest Exchange to hold their money while looking for new investments.

Soon after acquiring Southwest Exchange, McGhan, according to federal investigators, transferred $47.3 million from Southwest Exchange to MediCor. Just like that. Including $640,000 from Dennis, the avocado farmer.

Now I was on our corporate jet, en route to Las Vegas, on my way to help Dennis attempt the impossible.

I thought about McGhan and what it might be like to confront him face to face. At the time, I had no idea I was walking into a $100 million problem involving hundreds of investors. Or that McGhan was a bad guy, a criminal, presiding over a large-scale Ponzi scheme. All I knew was that this wasn't going to be pleasant.

As I drove to Henderson, a Las Vegas suburb, I had a strong sense of purpose. Not only was McGhan harming Dennis, not only was McGhan in the wrong, but the lost $640,000 also was holding up my Hawaii deal.

I pulled into the Southwest Exchange parking lot, and I met Dennis for the first time in person. He was a nice guy, looked like your typical farmer, and looked like a guy who really needed my help.

I was clearly nervous. Although I almost always enjoy pitching deals, it's usually for new business. Making this kind of pitch, to get money back—a lot of money—from a bad deal, is mentally and emotionally tough.

To calm myself, I thought about frame control and all the other methods that I had spent countless hours learning, and trying to master. As I mentioned before, no situation has real *meaning* until you frame it. *Frames* are mental structures that shape the way we see the world and put relationships in context. The frame you put around a situation completely and totally controls its meaning. But you aren't the only one framing. People are always trying to impose frames on each other. The frame is like a picture of what you want the interaction to be about. And the most powerful thing about frames? There can be only one dominant frame during any interaction between two people.

When two frames come together, the stronger frame absorbs the weaker frame. Then weak arguments and rational facts just bounce off the winning frame.

Dennis and I spoke for a few minutes in the parking lot. I prepared my frame. Then, just like that, I was ready, so we walked into the building together, and I went looking for the one guy who had caused all these problems: Donald McGhan.

It was 9 a.m. when we walked into the building. It was a generic looking office with a black leather couch and magazines spread neatly on the coffee table.

"Good morning. How can I help you?" a receptionist asked.

"I don't need help," I said. "Just tell me which office Don McGhan is in."

She began her gatekeeper script: "I'll see if he's in."

Rituals like these are meant to reinforce status hierarchies. But I was there to establish my own status and frame control and certainly not to supplicate a gatekeeper.

I strode past the front desk and down the hallway, the gatekeeper chasing behind me. She tried to keep me out of the office, to keep me from finding Dennis's money, so I had no choice but to start throwing open doors to various offices, interrogating anyone and everyone. What were they going to do, call the cops? Back at the office, my partner already had the local police and the FBI on speed dial.

"Where's Don McGhan?" I bellowed!

There were plenty of people now trying to stop me, but I wasn't going to stop until I'd spoken to McGhan. And I wasn't going to leave without Dennis's $640,000.

As I made my way through the building, office by office, Don McGhan hustled himself out the back door, not wanting to deal with me. Instead, he sent his son, Jim, who finally came out to "handle" things.

Jim McGhan, in his early 40s, was dressed in an Armani suit and had a confident, arrogant way about him. He was tall, and he looked down at me. We sat in a conference room, and right away, he was trying to take control, trying to frame things by saying, *There's a rational explanation for all of this.*

So *that* was his game; he was playing with the *analyst frame*, which relies on facts, figures, and logic.

I had a better frame prepared, the *moral authority* frame, and it's an analyst disruptor.

"Jim, you cannot hold Dennis's money," I told him. "We've requested it properly, and you're going to get it for him right now."

Jim was a player. I saw it in his eyes. But he knew that his scheme was falling apart, and he wasn't interested in giving Dennis the money. Instead, the money probably would be wired to McGhan's attorney by day's end, and then, we'd never get it. He knew what he was doing. He was using his status and authority to confidently explain the so-called facts.

I give him credit for one thing: Jim pulled off a beautiful analyst frame. He was completely unfazed, arrogant, and acting puzzled as to why we were there. Then he began with a rational, highly detailed, and analytical explanation of why the money couldn't be transferred right away.

This was the squaring-off phase.

He was trying to spin. He thought he could put us off and have us leave empty-handed.

Of course, I wasn't having that. I came in with a moral authority frame—that we were right and he was wrong—a nearly unshakeable frame when used correctly. The game was on. He knew my frame, and I knew his.

Next came the moment of first contact. It's that moment when two opposing frames are about to collide with full force. You can feel it—usually as a pang of anxiety in the pit of your stomach. It is at this moment when you need to strengthen your resolve and commit completely to your frame. No matter what happens, no matter how much social pressure and discomfort you suffer, you must stay composed and stick to your frame. This is called *plowing*. So you prepare yourself to plow, as an ox might plow a field. *Always moving forward. Never stopping. Never any self-doubt.* And, as you are about to see, when two frames collide, the stronger one always wins.

The niceties didn't last long. I spoke plainly and looked Jim right in the eyes. "We want Dennis's $640,000, and we are getting all of it back from you, today, right now."

He hemmed and hawed. He threw out a bunch of promises, half-truths, and MBA double talk. But I saw through the jibberish. And I had the stronger frame: *moral authority.*

I plowed.

"Look," I said. "Your lips are moving, but I'm not listening to a single word. Your words have no meaning. Stop talking. Start transferring money." He blinked. He tried one more time to explain, to argue, to rationalize why the money hadn't been transferred to Dennis, something about misplaced wire-transfer numbers. But rational explanations will never override a moral authority frame.

At one point, I saw the realization cross his face. He knew that he had picked the weaker frame. In fact, he tried the moral authority frame out for himself, "You know what, I've had enough of this. Get out of here now, or I'm going to call the cops."

But it was too late for him. He had already picked a weak analyst frame and had overcommitted to it—and was about to pay for
doing so. It was time for *frame disruption*. I was ready to pulver-
ize his frame into a puff of fine mist.

I pulled out my phone and dialed a colleague, Sam Greenberg.
I put him on speaker and discussed the logistics of getting the FBI
involved. Dramatic? Yes. But Jim McGhan knew at that moment
we were 100 percent committed to following through. I was acti-
vating the primal fears in his croc brain. As soon as he became
afraid, my frame would crush his, and he would bend to my will.

"Let me paint a picture for you, Jim," I told him. "You've seen
SWAT teams in the movies. It happens *just like that*. They are going
to swarm through this door, FBI accountants wearing Kevlar vests
and Glock 22s. And the sheriff will be blasting pepper spray at anything that moves, dogs will be barking, and they'll be fastening
your hands behind your back with zip ties. Is that how you want
today to end, hog-tied, pepper sprayed, lying in the back of a black
van with no windows? The other option is—you starting transferring money to us."

SMASH! That was the moral authority frame, delivered with
emotional realism, and here, I achieved the *hookpoint*. Our frames
had collided. My frame had absorbed his. The only options were
my options. There's a moment in games of strategy when the other
side realizes that no matter what moves it makes, the game is lost.
This was *that moment*.

I now had his full attention. Although it was his office and his
domain, I had the seized the high-status position. Although he still
had our money, $640,000, I had the *frame control*.

"Jim, starting right now, every 15 minutes, you're going to give
me a deliverable. That means—just so you understand me perfectly—
every 15 minutes something happens that benefits *me*. Cancel your

schedule, do not leave this room, pick up the phone, and start finding our money."

He was listening, and I continued.

"I need the money wired to Dennis's account, right now."

Just because you have frame control doesn't mean that someone won't push back. You *just stay committed to your frame and keep it strong. You plow.* Jim started with more MBA doublespeak, returning to rationalization mode. So I expanded the frame to include new characters and new consequences.

"Listen, Jim. *Stop*," I told him. "Get your friends and family and investor's list and start dialing for money. Every 15 minutes you need to hand me a wire-transfer confirmation."

This was the point of consolidation. Because I had done everything right, up to this point, there was no need to make threats or create drama. *The frame was set. The agenda was my agenda. Because the social interaction was being governed by my frame, these were the rules Jim had to follow:*

Rule 1: Everything happening must involve Dennis's money.
Rule 2: Something good must happen every 15 minutes.
Rule 3: The meeting isn't over until all $640,000 is wired.

I sat with Jim for six long hours as he dialed associates, family members, and friends. The money came rolling in, in small increments ($10,000 here, $15,000 here).

As I mentioned earlier, when two mental frames come together, when they collide, the stronger frame disrupts and absorbs the weaker frame. I'd controlled the frame, started it small, and expanded it, and Jim's weaker frame collapsed. His internal state went from nonchalance and arrogance to panic and desperation. His status went from high to low. Responding to my frame, he raised Dennis's money, and we walked out with all the $640,000—irrevocably secured via wire transfers. Mission accomplished.

Over the next few days, Dennis and I and some other victims worked with the authorities and Southwest Exchange was raided. I got Dennis's $640,000 out just in time, thanks to my knowledge of framing. Not for a moment was it about threats or power plays.

Although it was Dennis's money legally, perhaps Jim and Don McGhan never should have given back that $640,000. It wasn't in their best interests. If Jim McGhan really thought I was going to call the FBI, he should have wired that money to his attorney. It was clearly the last bit of cash Jim and Don could scratch together.

I had always respected the nature of frame control. But now, with Dennis's $640,000 back in my escrow account, I was learning to rely on it more and more often.

All told, the McGhans had bilked more than 130 investors out of more than $180 million. Several people lost their life savings, and the case spawned numerous lawsuits. In 2009, Don McGhan, age 75, was sentenced to a 10-year prison sentence for wire fraud.

This is an example of owning the frame. There are still more frames that you will encounter that I haven't discussed yet. Let's take a look at *time-based frames* and how to respond to them.

The Time Frame

Frames involving *time* tend to occur later in the social exchange, after someone has already established frame control. Again, if you want to know who has the frame, it's easy to observe. *When you are reacting to the other person, that person owns the frame. When the other person is reacting to what you do and say, you own the frame.*

Time frames are often used by your Target to rechallenge your frame by disrupting you and, in the moment of confusion, unwittingly take back control. As long as you are alert, time frames are easy to defeat.

You will know that a time-frame collision is about to occur when you see attention begin to wane. You've been pitching for a few minutes, and the temperature in the room is noticeably cooler. The game you initiated was fun at the beginning, and now the audience has cooled and might be a little bored. There are limits to the human attention span, which is why a pitch must be brief, concise, and interesting, as you will read about in Chapter 4.

If you wait for someone in the audience to say (or give body language to the effect), "We only have a few minutes left, so let's wrap this up," you will lose the frame because you now have to react to that person.

Instead, when you see attention begin to bottom out and expire, that's it. You're done. Stay in control of time, and start wrapping up. *Running long or beyond the point of attention shows weakness, neediness, and desperation.*

In Chapter 4, I explore attention extensively and you'll begin to understand that attention is an extremely rare cognitive phenomenon that is exceedingly difficult to create and manage. When attention is lacking, set your own time constraint, and bounce out of there:

"Hey, looks like time's up. I've got to wrap this up and get to my next meeting." If they are interested in you, they will agree to a follow-up.

Ironically, the mistake most people make when they see their audience becoming fatigued is to talk faster, to try to force their way through the rest of the pitch. *Instead of imparting more valuable information faster, however, they only succeed in helping the audience retain less of their message.* Here is another example of an opposing time frame and how to respond to it. If you visit customers' offices, you will recognize this situation:

CUSTOMER: "Hi, yes, um, well, I only have about 10 minutes to meet with you, but come on in."
SALESPERSON: "I really appreciate your time. Thanks for fitting me into your busy schedule."

This is a common dialogue and form of business etiquette—*and it is exactly the wrong thing to do.* You are reinforcing your target's power over you and confirming your target's higher status. You are essentially handing your target your frame and saying, "Here, please, crush my frame, control me, and waste my time."

When you encounter a time frame like this, quickly break it with a stronger prize frame of your own. Qualify your target on the spot.

YOU: "No. I don't work like that. There's no sense in rescheduling unless we like each other and trust each other. I need to know, are you good to work with, can you keep appointments, and stick to a schedule?"

YOUR TARGET: "Okay, you're right about that. Yeah, sure I can. Let's do this now. I have 30 minutes. That's no problem. Come on in."

You have just broken your target's time frame, established that your time is important, and he is now giving you focused attention instead of treating your visit like an annoyance.

Another frame that you will encounter is called the *analyst frame*. Like the time frame, the analyst frame usually appears after the initial frame collision and can derail you just when you are about to reach a decision. It is a deadly frame that you must know how to repel using the *intrigue frame*.

The Intrigue Frame

How many times have you been giving a presentation when suddenly one or more people in the room take a deep dive into technical details? That's the *analyst frame* coming at you. This is especially common in industries that involve engineers and financial analysts. This frame will kill your pitch.

The moment your audience does a "deep drill-down" into the minute details, you are losing control. The cognitive temperature of the audience, which was hot when things got started, naturally will cool as audience members listen to your pitch. But once you give their neocortex(es) something to calculate, they will go cold. *Problem solving, numerical calculations, statistics, and any sort of geometry are called* cold cognitions. Nothing will freeze your pitch faster than allowing your audience to grind numbers or study details during the pitch.

As you will learn in Chapter 4, the key to preventing this is to control access to details. Sometimes, however, a drill-down will happen anyway, and you have to act—fast.

It is important to realize that *human beings are unable to have hot cognitions and cold cognitions simultaneously.* The brain is not wired that way. *Hot cognitions* are feelings like wanting or desire or excitement, and *cold cognitions* come from "cold" processes like analysis and problem solving. To maintain frame control and momentum, you must force your audience to be analytical on its own time. You do this by separating the technical and detailed material from your presentation.

Oh, for sure, audience members will ask for details. They believe that they need them. So what should you do if someone demands details? You respond with summary data that you have prepared for this specific purpose.

You answer the question directly and with the highest-level information possible. Then you redirect their attention back to your pitch.

In financial deals, I respond with something like this:

"The revenue is $80 million, expenses are $62 million, the net is $18 million. These and other facts you can verify later, but right now, what we need to focus on is this: Are we a good fit? Should we be doing business together? This is what I came here to work on."

If you're pitching a product and the drill-down is on price, don't chase this conversation thread. Do answer fast, answer directly with high-level details only, and go straight back to the relationship question.

What this tells the audience is that (1) I'm trying to decide if you are right for me; (2) if I decide to work with you, the numbers will back up what I'm telling you, so let's not worry about that now; and (3) I care about who I work with.

Keep the target focused on the business relationship at all times. Analysis comes later. This is the best and most reliable way to deal with a target who suddenly becomes bored and tries to entertain himself with the details of your deal.

Remember, when you own the frame, you control the agenda, and you determine the rules under which the game is played.

There will be times when you are doing everything right, but for reasons beyond your understanding or control, the other person stops responding to you. The personal connection you had at one point seems to be fading.

When it no longer seems that communication is flowing back and forth, the other person is in something called a *nonreactive state*. It's like the other person's mind is wandering or thinking about something else. This is a state of disinterest that you can correct for if you recognize it in time and act quickly.

You can tell that this is starting to happen when you notice remarks or body language that indicate that your presentation is not intriguing—when the target thinks he can easily predict what your idea is before you even explain it or when he feels that he can anticipate what you are going to say and how you're going to say it.

Most intelligent people take great pleasure in being confronted with something new, novel, and intriguing. Being able to figure it out is a form of entertainment, like solving the Sunday puzzle. Our brains are wired to look for these kinds of pleasurable challenges.

When you described your idea initially to your target, you were pulling on a primal lever. When the target agreed to the meeting with you, what he or she really was saying was, "This is a puzzle I am interested in solving."

No one takes a meeting to hear about something they already know and understand. It's a fundamental concept driving every single presentation—it's the hook that allows you as the presenter to grab and hold attention by subconsciously saying, "I have a solution to one of your problems. I know something that you don't." This is why people agree to take meetings and to hear a pitch.

At the start of the meeting, you have the audience's attention. It's a rare moment, but not for the reason you may think. Audience members are, with full concentration and at the most basic and primal level, trying to figure out the answer to this question:

"How similar is your idea to something I already know about or to a problem I have already solved?"

If audience members discover that the answer is close to what they had earlier guessed, they will mentally check out on you. They will experience a quick ping of self-satisfaction at the moment of realization, just before they mentally *check out*.

But *checking out* is not just a catch phrase to describe drifting attention or wandering minds. Checking out, in this context, refers to something very specific: an *extreme and nearly total loss of alertness*, and this is exactly what you need to avoid.

As your pitch moves along, at any time, some or all members of your audience will solve the puzzle, see the solution, and *get* the whole story. Then they check out. This is why you see presenters lose more and more of the audience as time goes on—*those who solve the puzzle drop out.*

We generalize by saying, "Oh, they lost interest." But what really happened is that they learned enough about our idea to feel secure that they understand it—and there is nothing more to be gained by continuing to pay attention. They determined that there was no more value to be had by engaging with us on any level.

As I've said before, the brain is a cognitive miser. Unless it can get value for itself, it stops paying attention. The analyst frame can devastate your pitch because it only values hard data and ignores the value of relationships and ideas. This frame is completely lacking in any kind of emotion or connection to the people in the room.

The most effective way to overcome the analyst frame is with an *intrigue frame.* Of the four frame types at your disposal, intrigue is the most powerful because it hijacks higher cognitive function to arouse the more primitive systems of the target's brain.

Narrative and analytical information does not coexist. It cannot; that's simply impossible. The human brain is unable to be coldly analytical and warmly engaged in a narrative at the same time. This is the secret power of the intrigue frame.

When your target drills down into technical material, you break that frame by telling a brief but relevant story that involves you. This is not a story that you make up on the spot; this is a personal story that you have prepared in advance and that you take to every meeting you have. Since all croc brains are pretty similar, you will not need more than one story because the intrigue it will contain will have the same impact on every audience.

You need to be at the center of the story, which immediately redirects attention back to you. People will pause, look up, and listen because you are sharing something personal.

As you share your story, there has to be some suspense to it because you are going to create intrigue in the telling of the story by *telling only part of the story*. That's right, you break the analyst frame by capturing audience attention with a provocative story of something that happened to you, and then you keep their attention by not telling them how it ends until you are ready.

This is much more powerful than you may imagine. Now I can't give you a story to tell; that has to come from you. But what I can do is tell you what your story should contain and then tell you my personal analyst frame crusher so you can see how the elements come together to recapture and hold audience attention.

The Intrigue Story

Your intrigue story needs the following elements:

1. It must be brief, and the subject must be relevant to your pitch.
2. You need to be at the center of the story.
3. There should be risk, danger, and uncertainty.
4. There should be time pressure—a clock is ticking somewhere, and there are ominous consequences if action is not taken quickly.
5. There should be tension—you are trying to do something but are being blocked by some force.
6. There should be serious consequences—failure will not be pretty.

What's new here is not that you should tell some kind of story to your target. What's new and important is *when* to use it—as soon as you recognize that the target is coming at you with an analyst frame. Then use it to nudge him out of analytical thinking. There are half a dozen other ways to disrupt the analyst frame—anger and extreme surprise are two. But in most social situations they are impractical. The intrigue frame does it better and does it fast.

Here is my intrigue story, which I will tell you first, and then I will show you how I tell this story to my audience.

My Intrigue Story: The Porterville Incident.   Recently, I was traveling in our company plane with my business partner and our attorney. We were at an airstrip in Porterville, a small California town about 300 miles from San Francisco. While this tiny airstrip served mostly small local aircraft, jet traffic in the air was heavy because of the many commercial planes going in and out of San Francisco. A jet must make a rapid and steep ascent after takeoff to join in with the busy traffic pattern.

In a pitch setting, I do not tell this story the way I just relayed it to you. When I was meeting with officials from a local airport, I told this story much differently. Knowing that my audience was made up of aviators, engineers, and guys interested in jets, I came to the meeting with this story prepared and ready to deploy if needed. As it happened, I did encounter an attack from an opposing analyst frame, and this story easily brought the meeting back under my control.

As the audience's attention began to shift to analytical questions, this is what I said:

"This reminds me of the Porterville incident. A while ago, my partner and I flew to Porterville to look at two deals. You guys know, they have a tiny airfield; it's visual-flight-rules-only and has no control tower."

"Mostly they get single-engine traffic—Cessna Skycatchers and Beechcraft Bonanzas—and maybe a few small jets. So when we got there, our big Legacy 600 skidded to a stop at the far edge of the runway. But the landing was nothing compared with the takeoff.

"Since Porterville airspace is under San Francisco air traffic control, 260 miles away, the trick to getting out of there is to climb fast and merge quickly into the traffic pattern. We expected an aggressive takeoff. It was no big deal when we found ourselves accelerating hard into a steep climb.

"The Legacy 600 is a 'muscle car' of a jet. When it's under full power, you feel it. So we're heavy and deep in this full-power ascent, we're having casual business conversation, and I would estimate that our altitude was 9,000 feet when abruptly the jet surges and then *nosedives*.

"We dropped 1,000 feet in a few seconds.

"My seat is facing forward, toward the cockpit. The door is open, and I can see the pilots.

"We are all clinging to our seats and cursing, a Klaxon is howling, and one of the pilots is saying, 'It's the TCAS! It's the TCAS!' But I didn't even know at the time what a traffic collision-avoidance system was.

"I'm trying to figure this all out, and I'm thinking this is it— I'm done, *Soy un perdedor.* . . .

"As we're plummeting in this nosedive, I look through the door into the cockpit and see both pilots with their hands on the throttle. *Then* the plane rolls into a steep climb, *and I see the pilots fighting*, literally slapping each other's hands off the throttle. The climb is short—just five seconds—and then the plane goes into a *nosedive again*.

"Anyway . . ."

And I go right back into my pitch. Why does this strategy work so well? The most extreme explanation is that the audience becomes immersed in the narrative. They take the emotional ride with me. Sure, they know that we obviously survived, but I've piqued their curiosity—*why were the pilots fighting?* They want to know. When I do not tell them, the intrigue spikes high enough to shock them out of the analyst frame.

In my experience with this approach, the opposing analyst frame gets crushed by emotional, engaging, and relevant narratives like this. Attention redirects back to me, allowing me to finish my pitch on my agenda, my timeline, and my topics.

After I finish the pitch, I complete the narrative arc by explaining the whole story:

"It turns out that the sudden dive was caused by the traffic collision-avoidance software built into the autopilot system. It had detected another airplane flying into our ascent path, and the computer had taken evasive measures just in time to avoid a crash. This was a very close call, and I am fortunate to be able to share this story with you now.

"The reason the pilots were fighting over the controls was because the copilot did not know the computer had taken over. But the pilot, older and more experienced, knew this and was pulling the copilot's hands off the controls. The collision-avoidance software was doing its job."

This true story has everything I need in an intrigue story—it's brief; it has a tight timeline; it has danger, suspense, and intrigue (what were those pilots doing?)—and it happened to be perfectly relevant to a pitch I was making to the operators of an airport, which you will read about later.

Perhaps, in a broader sense, this is why we tell each other intriguing narratives—to participate in powerful emotional experiences involving high-stakes situations that we hope we will never have to face ourselves. A short, personal narrative like this is important to your audience because it reveals something about you, your character, and your life. As you think about your intrigue story, don't be afraid to make it very personal. As long as it's relevant to your business and has the six elements described earlier, it will serve you well.

Stop the Analyst Frame Cold

The key to using an intrigue frame is to trust in its power to stop the analyst frame cold. Remember, the person using the analyst frame will break your pitch into pieces and ultimately crush it if unchecked. The analyst frame filters your deal like this:

1. It focuses on hard facts only.
2. It says that aesthetic or creative features have no value.
3. It requires that everything must be supported by a number or statistic.
4. It holds that ideas and human relationships have no value.

Do not let your audience go there—keep audience members focused on the relationship they are building with you. Your intrigue story breaks this analyst rule set in an entertaining way and replaces analytical thinking with narrative discourse.

Breaking the Analyst Frame with Suspense

Consider the movie *Jaws* for a moment. This 1975 Steven Spielberg film is a classic, and decades later, it is still doing a brisk business on DVD. Why does this story work so well? In the first part of the film, Spielberg doesn't show you the shark. The great white lurks below the surface, creating a sense of terror and suspense. Where is it? When will it strike next? How big is it?

We see someone in the water, minding her own business. Then we see her as a victim, screaming, kicking, getting pulled under, and eventually disappearing in a froth of red water. This predator is unseen, and we have no idea when it's going to strike next. This creates great tension, and we are riveted to the action.

Now let's reimagine *Jaws*. Let's assume that the shark is fitted with a GPS transponder and that we know its exact location at all times. We know where the shark is going, where it's been, and what it looks like. When it comes time to hunt the shark, Police Chief Martin Brody and the crazy shark hunter, Quint, know exactly where to go and what they're up against.

Strapping a GPS transponder on the shark strips away the mystery and the intrigue. Telling the story this way would have wiped out nearly a billion dollars in box office revenue. *If you know where the shark is at all times, you have no tension, no suspense, no blockbuster.* The same can be said for your narrative.

Use the elements of surprise and tension, and as you approach the most interesting part of the story, move away from it and leave the audience *intrigued*—until *you* are ready to reveal. Clearly, this technique made Spielberg one of the most successful directors in history. It works for me in business settings, and it will work for you.

The Prizing Frame: Reloaded

Prizing is a way to deal with threatening and fast-approaching frames that are likely to push you into a low-status position. When you prize, you frame yourself as high value in the eyes of your target. Prize correctly, and your target will be chasing you.

Establishing a prize frame is the very first thing you need to do when you are on someone else's turf, ready to begin your pitch. When you get to the end of your pitch and it's time to get a deal, your success depends on how well you establish your frames at the beginning and how strong those frames actually are.

For a moment, think of the alternative to having strong frames. One is to sell harder by making more calls and being more pushy. In fact, our business culture has a fascination with the idea that a salesperson should never take no for an answer. There's pressure from the top. Always be chasing. Always be closing.

Everyone has heard a friend tell a version of this story: "The buyer didn't want my product, but I wouldn't take no for an answer. I just kept pounding away, until he finally signed up."

Such stories dramatize the myth that you can succeed by badgering your clients into buying something. The truth is, this rarely works, and when it does, you are sure to encounter buyer's remorse.

The same is true with pitching. If you think you can browbeat your target until finally he relents, you have it backwards.

Whenever we chase someone or value someone else more than ourselves, we assume the subordinate position and put ourselves at a disadvantage. Although we talked briefly about this before, I'll now introduce you in greater depth to the concept of prizing and the prize frame.

Who is the prize, or who is chasing whom, is one of the underlying social dynamics that influences most meetings. The answer establishes a person's motivation and tells us how they will probably behave in the meeting. The basics:

- If *you* are trying to win your target's respect, attention, and money, he becomes the prize.
- When *your target* is trying to win your attention and respect, you are the prize. (This, of course, is what you want.)

Prizing is the sum of the actions you take to get to your target to understand that he is a commodity and you are the prize. Successful prizing results in your target chasing you, asking to be involved in your deal.

Why Is Prizing Important?

Successful prizing restores calm and poise to the social interaction. You won't have to chase as hard or worry so much about impressing your target. But there's another important benefit. It reduces your feeling of needing to perform to get a reward. Consider the way people talk about a presentation—they often call it a "dog and pony show." This label evokes self-defeating imagery of you riding around in a circle on a pony. The only thing missing is rainbow suspenders and a clown nose.

Getting rid of those negative labels and ideas is an important step. When you are no longer performing for the money, the frame changes drastically.

Sure, it's easy to think that you have to earn the buyer/investor's approval to win the money. Especially when you're in the investor's office, on his turf, giving your pitch. The prize frame is the window through which you look at the world that allows you to see yourself as the prize: The money has to earn you, not the other way around. You're flipping the script.

Why Does Prizing Work?

Your pitch is first going to register in the target's croc brain. And as we discussed in Chapter 1, the croc brain would like to ignore you. But if you are dynamic enough—giving new and novel information—you will capture the croc's attention. Once that happens, the croc is going to have one of two primal reactions:

- Curiosity and desire, or
- Fear and dislike.

Breaking it down into such simple terms helped me to understand a crucial concept: If you trigger curiosity and desire, the croc sees you as something it wants to chase. You become the *prize*.

Let's consider three of the most fundamental behaviors of human beings:

1. We chase that which moves away from us.
2. We want what we cannot have.
3. We only place value on things that are difficult to obtain.

Are these universally valid laws that can be relied on in all social interactions? I think they are. And by now, you can see where I'm going with this. If you pitch in front of strangers, you know how easy it is to come across as a little too eager to do business. At the same time, you might make it seem too easy to get what you have. All your audience has to do is nod, and you will do everything else—it's too obvious that you're willing to do anything at all to make them happy.

The problem with this approach is that if it is true that people only value things that are hard to get, you are not hard to get. There's no challenge. Behaving this way means that you are failing to prize.

And if you're pitching for money, your problems can multiply. Framing money as the prize is a common error—and often a fatal one. Money is never a prize; it's a commodity, a means for getting things done. Money simply transfers economic value from place to place so that people are able to work together.

Prizing 201: Avoiding the Mistakes

The prize frame works only if certain conditions are fulfilled. In Prizing 101, you learned two basic ideas:

1. *Make the buyer qualify himself back to you.* Do this by asking such questions as, "Why do I want to do business with you?"
2. *Protect your status.* Don't let the buyer change the agenda, the meeting time, or who will attend. Withdraw if the buyer wants to force this kind of change.

Prizing 201 offers additional lessons beyond the previous learning:

1. There is a great temptation to use trial closes because we've all been told this is how selling should be done: "So, are we in the ballpark?" or "What do you think so far?" *Don't do it. This shows you as being too eager to get a deal done.* Anyway, trial closes are crude and ineffective.
2. Instead, take the time to step back, to withdraw. Work to control the underlying prize frame—then you don't have to push your ideas so hard. Instead of a trial close, you

might issue a challenge (do it with humor or it will feel forced): "So many buyers, yet only one of me. How are you going to compete for my attention." I left out the question mark for a reason—because you are not seeking validation from the target. You don't have to ask it as a question; just issue it as a statement. It's important to get used to making statements instead of asking questions. Doing it this way shows that you aren't constantly seeking validation.

3. Make the target perform a legitimate task to earn the deal. For example, BMW has a special-edition M3 that requires you to sign a contract promising you'll keep it clean and take care of the special paint. The company won't even let you buy one until you promise this in writing.

4. What follows might sound like advice from the positive-mental-attitude crowd, but it's an important part of the learning: The prize frame works best when you change your attitude about money—fully realizing that money is almost useless to any buyer/investor until it purchases what you have. Oh sure, the investor's money can earn a few bucks in Treasury bills or corporate bonds. But that's not what money wants to do. It wants to go to work by investing in deals and buying products. How does this work in the real world? This can seem a little abstract until you fully internalize the following fact: Money cannot do anything without you. The money needs *you*.

When you combine the elements in Prizing 101 and 201, at first it feels like you are walking up the down escalator. This is a natural reaction. Don't worry, prizing does not mean that we have given up the pursuit of buyers—that would be an absurd notion. It means we must give up the concept of ABC, or "Always Be Closing," a phrase popularized by the sales gurus of the 1980s. Instead, you must embrace the idea that money is a commodity, that it is available in a thousand places, and that it's all the same no matter where it comes from. Knowing this, it is more likely you will embrace ABL— "Always Be Leaving." And it's also likely that you'll embrace the money that comes with it.

Money is a commodity. Every investment banker and economist you'll meet will confirm this. Imagine that—Investors reframed as a commodity, a vending machine for money. When you think about it, this makes perfect sense because there are many places to source money, but there is only one you. Your deal is unique among all others. If you think of yourself and your deal in this way and build frames around this idea, you will be pleased at how it will change the social dynamics in your meetings with investors.

If you want to get started with this, in a simple, low-risk way, here is a phrase I often use to set the prize frame firmly in place: "I'm glad I could find the time to meet with you today. And I do have another meeting right after this. Let's get started." This is always a good start because it tells the audience that there are many like them but only one of you.

As you move into your pitch, find moments to reinforce the other frames you hold. For example, make appropriate comments about the value of your time to strengthen both your time frame and your prize frame.

If someone asks a question that is relevant yet veers toward an analytical tangent, let the question just bounce off your stronger power frame. Save the discussion of details for later, after you have said what you want to say.

Remember, small acts of defiance and denial, combined with humor, are extremely powerful in maintaining your frame control and in reinforcing your high status. Humor is important here—don't leave it out, or I guarantee that you will encounter unpredictable responses.

Chapter 3

Status

Status plays an important role in frame control. How others view you is critical to your ability to establish the dominant frame and hold onto the power you take when you win the frame collision. But most people in business and social interactions view status incorrectly. You don't earn status by being polite, by obeying the established power rituals of business, or by engaging in friendly small talk before a meeting starts. What these behaviors might earn you is a reputation for being "nice." They do nothing for your social position—except *reduce* it.

Another common mistake is underestimating the value of status. People confuse status with charisma or ego, which are entirely different things. And they mistakenly believe that working to raise one's social value is foolish or just an act of peacocking. Nothing could be further from the truth.

Unless you are a celebrity, a tycoon, or the guy who just landed your company the largest deal it has ever done, in most cases you enter a new business setting with a low social position. The harder you try to fit into this social scene, the lower your perceived social value becomes.

Yet fitting in and having high social status are essential. Every interaction is affected by pecking order—who is the dominant group member and who are the subordinates. And the moment you enter a room to pitch is a beautiful example of how the social animal inside you works. In those first moments, the alpha and beta social positions are up for grabs. But it's not a physical skirmish—it's the rapid and sometimes instant assessment of each other's social position. When it comes down to finding the alpha, nobody takes the time to draft a balance sheet of who owns the most assets, who commands the most wealth, and who is the most popular. It's a subconscious and instant recognition of status.

Within seconds, we each need to decide, for the sake of our own self-preservation, *who in this room is the dominant alpha?* And if it turns out that someone else is the dominant alpha and we are the beta, there is a second, even more valuable question: In the short amount of time we have to orient ourselves in this social interaction, *can we switch out of the beta position and take the alpha?*

People will judge your social status almost immediately, and changing their perception is not easy. But it's important because your social status is the platform from which you must pitch.

If you are pitching from a lower-level platform, or low social status, your ability to persuade others will be diminished, and your pitch will be difficult, no matter how great your idea or product. However, if you hold high social status, even on a temporary basis, your power to convince others will be strong, and your pitch will go easily.

What I am saying—and what I have proven to myself and to others—is that you can alter the way people think about you by creating *situational status*. Let's look at how situational status plays out in a familiar social structure, one we have all encountered at one time or another.

The French Waiter

French waiters are respected throughout the world for their skill in controlling social dynamics. From the moment you enter their world, they set the frame and control the timing and sequence events according to their wishes. They wipe your status instantly, redistribute it as they choose, and control the frame throughout the exchange. You regain control only after the check has been paid, the tip has been left, and you're ushered out the front door.

I watched the waiters work their frame magic a few years ago on a bustling boulevard in Paris. I stopped in at Brasserie Lipp on the Boulevard Saint-Germain-des-Pres. My waiter was Benoit, who started there busing tables and washing dishes and moved his way up to head waiter. His father worked at this famous Left Bank *boîfite* before and after World War II, and today, there is nothing about the history of this place that Benoit does not know.

Benoit can show you the table where Ernest Hemingway did much of his writing during the 1920s and can seat you there if he is feeling generous (and senses that you will be generous in return).

There is nothing Benoit cannot tell you about the menu—every dish, every ingredient, every method of preparation. But to ask questions about the menu is a mild insult. Instead, it's better to ask him to recommend something. The same goes for the wine list, which is even longer than the menu. This is his job. He is the expert within the walls of his restaurant.

I entered Lipp's with some friends I'd invited out for dinner. I was the host, so I carried myself with authority and high status.

After all, I was the paying customer about to drop a big wad of cash. I wanted the maître d' and waitstaff to understand my status and give me the best they had to offer. The maître d' gave me a practiced look that said, *Yes, I know your kind. You're all the same to me.*

The restaurant was starting to get busy, but it was not full. We wouldn't have to wait long. The maître d' looked down at his schedule and intoned, "It will be a few minutes while we prepare your table, monsieur. Please wait here." Yet he didn't move. He looked down, scribbled a note on his seating chart, and began to ignore me.

Fifteen minutes passed. I watched as the best tables began to fill. I looked at the maître d', anxious, and he held up his index finger indicating *only a minute more.* I returned to my guests, defending my choice of restaurant and commenting on how good the food is.

"I promise you, it will be worth the wait," I told them.

Finally, when the right amount of time had passed, the maître d' stepped away from his podium and said, "Madames et messieurs, your table is ready," waving us toward our table with an open palm and outstretched arm.

He seated us, handed us menus, and told us that Benoit would soon arrive to take our orders. A trainee brought water and bread, smiled, and then disappeared.

Another 15 minutes ticked by before Benoit appeared, and the first thing he did was flash me a rebellious look. "Do you know what you would like to drink?" he asked, looking at the hand-tooled leather-bound *carte du vin* (wine list) resting near my left hand. I didn't recognize many wines on the list, so I played the part of good host and ordered an expensive bottle for the table.

This was Benoit's opportunity to perform a small but defiant act and to seize control of the high-status position, taking it away from me. You almost could hear the power transfer, clean and smooth, like the flip of switch:

"Hmm, monsieur, I do not think this wine is the best choice," he grimaced, taking the wine list away from me.

Benoit turned the page and paused. I was embarrassed, and my face turned red. "While all the wines in our cellar are fine wines, you must select a better pairing for this evening's meal," he said. He scanned our table, making eye contact with my guests, ignoring me.

He suggested various meals for my guests and, after several minutes, finally returned his attention to me. He flipped open the *carte du vin*, stabbing his index finger at a wine that would meet his standard. His recommendation was less expensive than the wine I had chosen. So I gave up on my selection and gave the nod to his.

"An excellent choice, monsieur," he announced to the table, pretending to the group that it was my knowledge—and not his— that resulted in the best choice. I was the butt of the joke, and my guests had a fun laugh.

Benoit flashed me a look that said, *This table is mine!*

The wine arrived, and Benoit carried out the time-honored ritual of corking, testing, and decanting. He executed the steps with precision, tradition, and respect for his craft. My guests were in awe. Only when it had been established that the wine would meet his exacting standards did he offer me, the host, the first taste.

At this point, he could have served me stale vinegar, and I would have said that it was heavenly, just to save face.

I wasn't sure whether I was angry with Benoit or just amused that he had turned me into a low-status dork. Benoit had simply and effectively grabbed *local star power.*

He had captivated the attention of the table, and now, in full possession of the social power that I once had, he decided to redistribute some of this power to further strengthen his position with my group.

As Benoit settled into a smooth rhythm of frame controls and status moves, I could see the game unfolding perfectly: acts of small defiance; seizing status, redistributing it; taunting me to behave like a beta. I was at the center of a master class on frame control.

As the wine was poured around the table, one of my guests smelled her wine and asked, "Is this a Bordeaux?" Benoit stood tall, placed a hand on her shoulder, and said, "Madame clearly knows French wine. This Bordeaux is from a small *terroir* that most people mistake for Langedoc. Your palate is very sophisticated." This comment absolutely melted her, and her eyes were sparkling with emotional pyrotechnics. The table was smiling, and again, I was ignored.

Let's pause to review what Benoit, this practiced master of social frame control, had accomplished. First, he seized local star power by using simple, seemingly innocent and benign acts. And he isolated me by making me wait.

As I discussed earlier, the croc brain is a social organ that craves acceptance and belonging. No one likes being made an outsider, especially when there are guests to impress.

Then, after ostracizing me, Benoit swooped in, using his superior domain knowledge, and made me look like a fool. He then quickly rescued me from a "mistake" he had allowed me to make.

He knew that without first understanding what kind of food the table would be ordering, it would be impossible to order the wine. And yet he asked me to make a wine selection first. No matter what I ordered, my order would be wrong. *Thanks, Benoit!*

He called out my mistake and then quickly polled the table for the information needed to make the correct decision. He chose the correct wine, making sure it was a better wine at a lower price than I had chosen, and then gave me credit for making the proper choice. This was an early masterstroke that secured his control of the social power he had taken from me two minutes earlier.

His next move was to strengthen his position by co-opting one of my guests into his frame, making it impossible for me to attack him without simultaneously attacking her.

He waited for someone to comment on the wine—anyone, any comment—and lavished praise on them to distribute some of his social power to that person. When one person joins his frame, the others will follow. And now the table was his. *Voilà!*

Back to the dinner. As expected, the entrees were superb, and Benoit suggested a second bottle of wine, something a little different to capture the flavors coming from the progressing meal. Benoit appeared more regularly now, floating around the table, collecting information, making suggestions, and basically doing the hard work of protecting his superior social position. My guests told me that this was one of the best meals they'd ever had. I thanked them for joining me and then gave Benoit an appreciative nod. At first, I wanted to smack Benoit, but now I was really starting to like him.

As the plates were cleared, Benoit disappeared. I had an expectation that something more was coming, but what? Ten minutes went by. Where was Benoit? I knew something was up.

I was right about that. Benoit had chosen the dessert. Moments later, a gleaming silver cart was rolled to our table, followed by a cart lined with brandy and cigars. Behind all this was the coffee cart—the attendant filled individual French press cylinders with freshly ground coffee.

"Madames et messieurs, for this evening's dessert, I have taken the liberty of making something special for you," Benoit announced. What he meant was, "I have taken over your host's mind and bank account."

"*Baba de rhum,*" he continued, "our most famous dessert, a light and delicious cake made with cream, rum, and a little sugar. Please enjoy."

The table applauded, and Benoit cut the cake with flair. I was so owned by Benoit at this point that it really no longer mattered. I smiled, relaxed, and decided that Benoit was going to get the largest tip he'd ever seen. In fact, the tip is the only power I had left in this situation.

My guests were delighted, and now, as the evening closed over coffee and brandy, Benoit slowly released some social power back to me. For a very good reason: The check was coming, and I was sure it would melt my neocortex.

"Madames et messieurs, it has been our pleasure to serve you this evening," Benoit gushed. He deftly placed a small silver tray near my left arm. On the tray was a tiny slip of paper turned face down, held in place by a small silver fleur-de-lis paperweight. No itemized bill could possibly fit on this miniscule slice of paper, just a single number would be on it. As my guests warmly thanked Benoit with hugs and handshakes, I managed a peek at the bill, flipping up the corner, like a poker player, not wanting to show any reaction.

It wasn't as bad as I thought.

With the performance Benoit gave, and the control he held throughout the evening, I was expecting him to take advantage. He had the power to do so, but in a final display of total frame control, he chose moderation over self-indulgence. Now I was absolutely delighted, and the large tip I was thinking of leaving him was just raised.

Alpha and Beta

It doesn't matter how well you argue, the way your points are crafted, or how elegant your flow and logic. If you do not have high status, you will not command the attention necessary to make your pitch heard. You will not persuade, and you will not easily get a deal done.

As you are now starting to realize, pitching any kind of idea or deal involves playing a complex and tricky status game. And before I talk about the ways to win the game, and possible ways to lose it as well, I should cover the real advantages held by the person with the highest status, the *alpha*. The alpha enjoys most of the attention in a social interaction, even when he's not demanding it. And when he *does* demand it, the alpha captures the group's attention immediately. When he makes a statement, it's regarded as true, and the claims go unchallenged. There's plenty of evidence to suggest that the alpha in a group is trusted and followed without question. To illustrate this, researchers have set up many tests in which men, dressed in high-status business suits, jaywalk across a busy street when it's unsafe to cross. Lower-status pedestrians tend to follow the high-status decoy into the danger zone. They will not follow someone who is dressed badly, however.

When you take the high-status position in a social interaction, you *feel it*, and it is also felt by your audience. Do not underestimate the importance and value of status to your overall success.

For more than 40 years, sales trainers have been teaching techniques and methods that help "situationally disadvantaged" salespeople (read: those with low social value) get an appointment, establish a temporary relationship (called *building rapport*, which contributes absolutely nothing to your social rank), package a business transaction in a thin and fragile emotional wrapper, and sometimes, if they're either lucky or doggedly persistent, close a sale.

During the 1970s and 1980s, these techniques worked, but even then, only for the most tenacious, hard-driving, type A personalities. Still, the purveyors of process-based sales methods continue training millions of ambitious salespeople in seminars from coast to coast. Today it's difficult to find an executive who isn't familiar with techniques like building rapport, pushing features and benefits, overcoming objections, and trial closing.

As a consequence, after generations of this process-driven business behavior, targets know how the sales game is played. *Use this stuff, and they will see it coming.* Even the best of these techniques are now so commonplace that clients have developed strong defenses and barriers to block them. These defenses are called *beta traps*, meaning that you are held in a subordinate position to the target (or buyer) at all times. You are *PWNED* from start to finish.

There is no substitute for holding a position of high status. The good news is that you need not be a celebrity or a billionaire to enjoy high levels of social status. There are ways you can create it instantly. And with it, you can capture and hold the attention of any audience or target.

The first step toward elevating your social status is to avoid the beta traps.

Beta Traps

In social interactions and business meetings as in nature, those who hold the dominant alpha rank are able to accomplish more than those holding a lesser rank. Alphas call the shots, give the orders, and create the outcomes they want with a minimum of effort. It's important to them emotionally and economically to remain the highest-ranking person in their social group.

Because they occupy a coveted rank, alphas have to constantly fight to maintain and protect their position. As top dog, their rank is under constant threat, and alphas protect themselves by asserting their authority over their employees and coworkers. They ask subordinates to run their errands, bring them coffee, and deal with matters that are disinteresting to them or are deemed to be below their rank. These are the nicer forms of dominant turf-protecting behaviors; many who hold alpha rank behave in far worse ways.

To shield themselves from people of higher social rank who visit them in their work environment, they erect a protective ring of social barriers intended to deflect and demote any threatening alphas.

A beta trap is a subtle but effective social ritual that puts you in the low-status position and works to keep you there, beneath the decision maker you have come to visit, for the entire duration of the social interaction. Most business environments are surrounded by a moat of beta traps that you already recognize and know: the reception desk, the lobby, the conference room, and any public meeting space in or near the office.

The first beta trap you encounter is the lobby. It's a venue created to welcome visitors, right? In fact, the lobby serves to demote you from the moment you arrive and keep you demoted throughout your visit.

You know the drill; how many times have you experienced this scenario?

You enter the lobby of the office where you will be meeting your target. You approach the reception desk. The receptionist looks up—"Hi, can I help you?"—then takes a call before you can answer. You stand, wait, and take a business card from the tray on counter. The receptionist transfers a call and then looks at you. "Yes? Can I help you?"

You say, "I'm here to see Bill Jones for a 2 o'clock. I talked to you earlier, I think, and you confirmed. ..."

The receptionist looks past you. "Sign the visitor's book, please. Here's your visitor's pass. Keep it with you at all times. Please take a seat. Bill's assistant will come get you in a few minutes." She then turns to finish a text message. You take a seat in the lobby. A table filled with dog-eared trade magazines and week-old newspapers indicate that others like you have been here before.

This sequence, in translation, reads as follows: Be a well-behaved salesperson, do as you're told, and you shall be rewarded with a bottle of water, a short visit, and a vague promise to "review your materials and information" after you leave. When you observe office power rituals, you are signaling to your target that you are a beta.

At 2:10 p.m., a young aide approaches you. "Hi. Yes, Bob is running a little late, shouldn't be more than another 10 minutes. Water and coffee are over there. Help yourself." You blink, she's gone.

Your target arrives late, offering a mock apology for his impossible schedule, telling you that he now has only a few minutes and still hasn't had a chance to review your materials. And now the decision maker, "Mr. Big," won't be able to attend the meeting as planned. Sorry. *At this point, you have been beta trapped and are completely and utterly defeated. You may as well go home.*

What a demoralizing way to do business. Yet this is how millions of people set and conduct business meetings. It's a waste of time because the behaviors and outcomes are so predictable and so unproductive.

Another common beta trap is the conference room. If it's empty when you arrive, you are usually left alone for several minutes, cooling your heels while you wait for your targets to arrive. When they arrive, the mood is often jovial, with lots of light social chatter, smiles, and handshakes. They are happy because they are now taking a break from their daily work to come into a nice, larger room to see today's entertainment—that's you. Who isn't happy when they step into a circus tent and take a seat at ringside? They know a show is about to start, and they're looking forward to relaxing and having a good time.

As you wait for the latecomers—the decision makers you really need in the room—conversations are now taking place that do not include you. Others talk to each other as if you were not in the room, which is not only annoying, but it's also one of the most degrading things one person can do to another. In this situation, you are the jester in another king's court, and your value is purely based on the quality of your entertainment. You have no status whatsoever.

Then there are public spaces where customers sometimes decide to take a meeting. "Let's get a coffee and talk," they say, leading you into a cafeteria or close-by café where you exchange small talk in the queue and manage an awkward moment over who should pay for the drinks. You take a place at a nearby table, within earshot of a dozen strangers. This is no place for a pitch.

Your status level is zero. You are owned, processed, and now are nothing but a pleasant social interlude in an otherwise boring day. But you press on, believing in yourself, and your offering. You open your pitch and are moving along nicely when suddenly some-one walks up to your customer and starts talking to him as if you do not exist. "Hey, Jim, how's it going?" the intruder says, shak-ing his hand and ignoring you. "Did you get my e-mail about the shipping delays in Dallas?" They continue their conversation for a while as you can do nothing but stare.

Eventually, when he decides he needs to go bother someone else, the intruder leaves, and your customer turns back to you. His face is blank, his eyes are empty, and his brain has stopped func-tioning. "Where were we?" he asks.

Need I go on?

There have been many frame collisions in this interaction—but you didn't win a single one of them. You have no control over the situation.

In general, public spaces are the most deadly beta traps and should be avoided. For a real pitch, coffee shops are an absolute last resort. I will mention one more public beta trap because it's common: trade shows and conventions.

If you exhibit at trade shows, you know that the absolute worst possible venue for pitching a customer is in a tiny booth or even on the convention floor. There are so many distractions that not even a frame-control ninja could hold an audience's attention for more than a few minutes without being interrupted by noise, announcements, or throngs of bag-carrying conventioneers mindlessly gathering free items to fill their brightly colored sacks.

If you need to pitch someone attending a conference, rent a hospitality suite or a hotel conference space or borrow someone's office conference room—pitch anywhere but on the floor of the convention hall.

A person standing in a trade show booth may as well erect a neon sign above his or her head that reads, *"I Am Needy!"* Like a caged pet-shop puppy or a late-night infomercial host, you try to draw them into your 8- by 10-foot cube and hope to wow them with your pitch. It's sad.

Beta Trapping in Bentonville.   In the town of Bentonville, Arkansas, the art of beta trapping has been taken to an unparalleled level. You might call it the "Frame Supercollider."

The world leader in the design, construction, and operation of beta traps is Walmart. At its headquarters in Bentonville is the world's most efficient salesperson-grinding apparatus you will ever see. No matter what you have to offer the company, no matter how great its value, to do business with Walmart, you must submit to a process that is designed to beat you down and wipe out your status, all in the name of lower prices.

Think I'm exaggerating? Go to 702 Southwest Eighth Street in Bentonville. Walk into the lobby. There you will find two enormous reception desks, one on each side of the room, with a hospitality area on the far right filled with grade school–style chairs with writing desks attached to them for those who need to fill out forms.

The perimeter of the room is lined with junk-food vending machines for those who need a quick energy boost to endure what is coming.

Between the two reception stations is a gleaming blue hallway marked with the Walmart logo that leads to another long hallway lined with dozens of six- by eight-foot meeting rooms. These meeting rooms are equipped with a door, one window, one small table, and four small plastic chairs. These rooms are where Walmart buyers meet with vendors.

Let's take a look at the company's process. First, you sign in, receive a visitor's badge, and are told to wait in the lobby. You are welcome to enter the company's hospitality room, and you can purchase candy and Walmart-branded soft drinks from the vending machines. The person you are visiting receives a message that you are in the lobby. When the buyer is ready to meet, you are paged to the reception desk and walked back to an assigned meeting room, where you are instructed to wait for your buyer to appear. As you are escorted to your assigned meeting room, you are allowed to see other vendors through the small glass windows of their cells. When you reach your cell, you are instructed to remain in the room until you are escorted out. Finally, the door is closed.

Eventually, one or two buyers will enter the cell, and your meeting will begin. The meetings are short and focused on price, volume, logistics, your financial ability to support the Walmart account, and then price again. Price is methodically and systematically driven down, whereas your logistical and product-support responsibilities are increased until you can no longer negotiate. When this point is reached, the Walmart buyers make a decision (buy or not) and move on to the next item in the product category.

The frame is so tightly controlled that even the most successful selling techniques do you absolutely no good. Walmart turns everything into a commodity, and every commodity is acquired through this process. Using scale, magnitude, and domination psychology for purchasing, Walmart has created the most effective frame supercollider in the history of free enterprise.

This is an extreme example of how beta trapping strips you of your power and ability to do good business. Old-fashioned sales techniques can help, but you are disadvantaged, you do not control the frame, and you are at the mercy of the buyer.

To compensate, you would need an enormous amount of self-confidence and self-belief to be convincing enough to succeed. You are forced to browbeat, manipulate, and cajole targets into buying decisions, and this is precisely why conventional sales methods focus on pressure closing.

Most of us don't have the required stamina and chutzpah—I certainly do not—and it's emotionally draining to have to make 100 sales calls to win an order or two.

When you are held down in beta position, the only tool you have at your disposal is emotional manipulation. At best, it works in the moment, and maybe you can land a deal. But your success is random, and it's not satisfying because the buyer really does not want to buy. He is doing so to please you now and will regret it later (buyer's remorse).

There is a much better and more natural way to attract business opportunities. You simply elevate your social value, and it's easier to do than you might think.

The Cardiac Surgeon and the Golf Pro.   Most golf professionals make their living by teaching the game, running golf clubs, operating golf courses, and dealing in golf equipment—not by caddying for touring professionals, like Phil Mickelson. In the United States, the label *golf pro* means an experienced golfer who helps other golfers with their game. It's a fun job. In many ways, being a golf pro is a dream job. You're working outside, teaching people a sport, and getting paid for it. The catch? It doesn't pay well. And

the golf pro or the French waiter, use your domain expertise and locational knowledge to quickly take the high-status position.

If you are meeting in the target's domain—his (or her) office or at an off-site location—you must neutralize the person holding high status, temporarily capture his star power, and redistribute some of his status to others in the room who will support your frame.

I have given you two examples of situational status and how to capture local star power. Now let's look at how you can elevate your status when your target is coming at you with the power frame.

The Hedge Fund Manager

A couple of years ago, I took a meeting with Bill Garr, a hedge fund manager. The meeting was arranged by a mutual friend, Dan. Arriving a few minutes early, I checked in with the receptionist and immediately recognized the lobby beta traps. Sign the guest book, here's your visitor badge, take a seat, and how about a stale cup of coffee? Someone will attend to you shortly.

Looking around the lobby, I made a quick read of the situation. Green marble floors, modern chrome and leather furniture, rich accents, all designed to convey a single message—I'm rich, I'm powerful, fear me, *revere* me. I knew what this was. I was on a conveyor belt headed straight for a status-crushing machine. Soon, my forehead would be stamped "Beta," and I'd have a 15-minute meeting with Bill and then would be shown the door. I knew instinctively that our first frame collision would not yield power to me. While I waited for Bill, I began to think of another way to acquire high status and take control of the frame.

Eventually, an assistant ushered me back to Bill's corner office. The level of luxury had been taken up a notch. His private office made the lobby look like a construction trailer. Teak furniture,

Persian rugs, titanium and glass fixtures, a couple of dozen framed pictures of Bill with various politicians and celebrities, and from his windows, a panoramic view of Beverly Hills that rivaled the view from Mulholland Drive.

"Have a seat," Bill said, without looking up from a document he was reviewing at his desk. I took a seat at the conference table by the window. "No, come over here," he said, pointing to a low-slung Eames chair in front of his desk. *The secretary's chair*, I thought to myself as I took the seat.

Bill was old school and enjoyed using classic power rituals like seating people below him to confirm his position as Lord William. I began to feel excitement because I have learned that the bigger they think they are, the harder they fall when my hookpoint is set. But I could sense that it was going to be a real challenge to get there.

Bill pressed a button on his phone and said, "Gloria, please ask Martin and Jacob to step in." A moment later, two smart-looking Ivy League MBAs came trotting in, taking subordinate seats on either side of mine. *I'm surrounded*, I thought. *Points for style, Bill.*

Bill reached into a rare Jean Cocteau ceramic bowl sitting on his credenza and plucked out a large red apple. As he did, he asked me to hold on another moment while he asked Gloria to e-mail someone he had forgotten to call. Turning back to me and his underlings, he propped one foot against a desk drawer and took a large bite from his apple. He set it on his desk while he searched for a napkin, and that was when I saw my first opportunity.

While he was chewing on his bite of fruit, I tried to get some kind of frame control. "Look, guys, I only have 15 minutes, so I'm going to get right to it. This is the deal I'm working on," and I quickly briefed the group on the project. But this frail attempt didn't accomplish much. The status gap between us was too big to overcome with just frame control. I could see that Bill was hearing every third word—he was more interested in his apple than in the opportunity I'd come to offer. I made a good opening and my pitch was progressing, but my status was still too low to have any chance at getting this deal to the closing table.

I'm good at this stuff, I said to myself. *Don't force an error. Wait for it.*

That was when I saw the golden opportunity. After years of dealing with similar—but not as difficult—social situations, the idea formed in my head, and I knew how to crush his frame, captivate his attention, and establish high status for myself with one simple move.

I said, "I need a glass of water. Excuse me" and raced for the kitchenette I had seen on the way in. There I grabbed a glass of water, a paper towel, and a plastic knife. I thought, *If this doesn't work, Bill is going to grab this knife and kill me with it.*

I walked back in but didn't sit. I said, "Listen, Bill, I hope that isn't how you do deals," nodding toward the apple that already had a bite out of it.

"In a real deal, everyone needs a piece. I'll show you what *my* deals look like."

I reached for the apple on the desk. "May I?" Not waiting for an answer, I took the apple, cut it in two, and took half for myself.

As I returned the half-apple to the place on the desk where Bill had set it, you could hear the roar of silence. The do-boys Martin and Jacob were stunned, and Bill was staring at me with mean and squinty eyes. I took a bite of apple, chewed it quickly, complimented its flavor, and commented a little more on how our deals always have been split fairly with investors. Then I finished the pitch, acting as natural and as informal as if I were having a conversation in my living room with friends.

The three of them listened to every single word from that moment on. I focused intently on the parts of the deal in which

I had expertise. Like Benoit or the golf pro, I was working hard to establish local star power.

When I had finished, and before Bill could speak, I quickly began to pull away. "Whoa, look at the time," I said a little comically, glancing at my watch, "I've got to run. Listen, guys, thanks for your time today. If this works for you, let me know."

As I reached for my folio and began to slide out of the chair, Bill waved his arm in the air and said, "Wait, wait. Wait a minute, Oren." And then he started hysterically laughing. This relieved the tension for Martin and Jacob. They smiled and laughed nervously with their boss, and I sat as straight-faced as I could while Bill got the huge laugh out of his system.

"I can definitely see why Dan said I should meet with you. Listen, tell me again who else you have in this deal."

The hookpoint was made. For the next 20 minutes, I answered questions and exchanged information with Martin and Jacob, who were tasked with the due diligence, and I continued pulling away, looking at my watch, worried about arriving late to my next meeting.

Finally, I stood up to leave. As I was shaking Bill's hand, he said, "If Marty and Jake tell me the numbers check out, I'm in."

What this example demonstrates is that a well-chosen, well-timed friendly but disruptive act will dethrone the king in a single stroke. In that brief, shocking moment when no one is quite sure what you've just done, that is when your frame takes over and when high status transfers to you.

To keep my frame strong, after the apple thing, I just ignored anything that didn't advance the pitch. This is an important lesson. In general, just ignore conversation threads that don't support your deal, and magnify ones that do. I kept talking about the deal—you'll see specifically some of the things I talked about in Chapter 4.

Here is a quick review of what happened in Bill's office that day:

1. I found myself in Bill's office with no frame control and in the beta position.
2. I perpetrated a mildly shocking but not unfriendly act that caused a new frame collision.
3. As the shock of my action wore off, the attention of the targets did not waver—believe me, it never does when you do something like this—and I continued accumulating status like a video gamer collecting power stars as each of the targets advances to new levels. The faster you grab status, the more is available for you to take.
4. As I captured attention, I then shifted my focus to acquiring local star power and the alpha status.
5. I got local star power by using information dominance to quickly shrink the frame around my area of specialization, making me unassailable. Because I was the expert, no one could undermine my deal points.
6. Using my newly acquired local star power, I quickly moved the discussion to a level where I could not be challenged by using the primary core values of hard work, domain expertise, and moral authority—which we will discuss in a moment.
7. The moment I was done with my pitch, I began to pull away and kept pulling away until I finally left the office—but not before I had set the hookpoint and received a decision.

These rules are applicable to any situation where you are pitching on someone else's territory.

Here are some other important things to remember:

- If you think you'll start a meeting from the beta position, always be on time for the appointment. When you are late, you are giving away power. It's difficult to establish strong frames when you can't play the game of business by its most basic rules.
- Momentum is key. Create high status immediately. Do not hesitate. Choose a frame, and force a collision at the most opportune moment—and do it early. The longer you wait, the more you reinforce the status of your target.
- Avoid social rituals that reinforce the status of others. Idle social banter diminishes your status.
- Have fun. Be popular. Enjoy your work. There is nothing as attractive as someone who is enjoying what he or she does. It attracts the group to you and allows you to build stronger frames and hold them longer.

As we have been saying, when you are the high-status person in a social interaction, you get all the good stuff. When you're the alpha, life is easy. The statements you make are trusted. The emotions you show will set the overall mood in the room. And most important, when you speak or gesture or even look like you *might* speak or gesture, people turn their attention toward you.

Just remember, this process is geared to build and seize situational status, which is temporary. Once you leave the social encounter, it's wiped out. Gone. And if you come back later, you'll have to start over and build it again. Even if that's only five minutes later.

And you won't be able to seize global status, which is the honor or prestige attached to a person's position in society. It's the sum of the person's wealth, popularity, and power. For example, you're not going to sit down with a billionaire and have him believe that you're somehow a triple billionaire. Global status is fixed. It's only situational status that you can grab and control.

Fortunately, you do not need to be rich, famous, or powerful to enjoy status in your business encounters and social situations. If you do not have high status, you can create it temporarily.

Seizing Situational Status

Here are the steps involved in elevating your status in any situation. You will recognize some of these actions from framing, and for good reason. Frame control and status are closely related, as are the pitch techniques you will learn in Chapter 4.

1. Politely ignore power rituals and avoid beta traps.
2. Be unaffected by your customer's global status (meaning the customer's status inside and outside the business environment).
3. Look for opportunities to perpetrate small denials and defiances that strengthen your frame and elevate your status.
4. As soon as you take power, quickly move the discussion into an area where you are the domain expert, where your knowledge and information are unassailable by your audience.
5. Apply a prize frame by positioning yourself as the reward for making the decision to do business with you.
6. Confirm your alpha status by making your customer, who now temporarily occupies a beta position, make a statement that qualifies your higher status.

The last step in this sequence is of vital importance, and it's not as scary as it sounds. As I pointed out earlier in this book, I do not abuse the power I am holding by committing overt acts of dominance. Instead, I am playful, with lots of give and take that makes doing business fun.

One of the best ways to get a customer to confirm your alpha status is to make him defend himself in a light-hearted way. Not only does this let you know that you are still in control, but more important, it also reminds the customer that he holds a subordinate position. The customer then will defer to you, even in front of his underlings.

I may say something like, "Remind me again why in the world I want to do business with you?"

This usually elicits a few guffaws—and a serious response amid the laughter: "Because we're the largest bank in California, Oren."

To which I say, "Yeah, that's good, I'll keep that in mind."

It needs to be playful and interesting, with just a little edge to it. Keep the customer qualifying back to you as long as you can. Do it as much as possible right up to the point where it becomes a little awkward—or is just taking too much time. Ask another qualifying question: "Have you ever done a deal this large before?" This is the best way I've found to get an audience to qualify my dominant frame.

Now that you have an understanding of frames and how to create and use status to support frame control, let's move on to the heart and soul of my method—the pitch.

Chapter 4

Pitching Your Big Idea

In 1953, molecular biologists James Watson and Francis Crick introduced the world to the double-helix DNA structure, the so-called secret of life, widely considered the most important scientific discovery of the twentieth century. The presentation earned Watson and Crick the Nobel Prize. And what is most striking about this accomplishment is that the full presentation takes just five minutes to read aloud. That's the *complete presentation*—introducing the secret of life, explaining it in detail, and showing how it works.

Pause and consider this for a moment: *The most important scientific discovery of the twentieth century can be pitched in five minutes.* Yet nearly every pitch that I've seen—and I see hundreds every year—takes at least 45 minutes and usually an hour, *a ridiculous amount of time!* No company in America should let's its executives pitch for an hour. In a moment, you'll see why.

Pitching the Big Idea

So far we have worked in the realm of frames and status, which are abstract notions. Now, however, lace up your shoes and tuck in your shirt—it's time to get in front of someone and deliver a pitch.

And if you're the front man, the guy who has to take a big idea on the road and pitch it, you need to know exactly how to give a complete presentation in a much shorter time frame than most. But as you'll see in a moment, short time frames are not a choice. You can't afford to run longer. The audience's brain won't give you more time. And worse, when attention runs dry—after about 20 minutes—the brain starts forgetting things it has already learned. Talk about going in reverse.

As soon as the pitch or presentation begins, one critical thing must happen: The target must feel at ease. In the vast majority of cases, they don't *because they don't know how long they're going to be stuck listening to you*, and you're a stranger. Most people just don't want to sit through an hour-long pitch. To put them at ease, I have a simple solution: It's called the *time-constraint pattern*. This is what you say, exactly, to let the target know he isn't trapped in the typical hour-long-meeting: "Guys, let's get started. I've only got about 20 minutes to give you the big idea, which will leave us some time to talk it over before I have to get out of here."

Doing it this way puts the target at ease. It shows that you know what you're doing and that you're a pro. *Anything* can be pitched in 20 minutes by a pro. It also shows that you're busy because you have a strong idea and you can't hang out too long in a single meeting.

What's important here is not your mastery over the details but your mastery over attention and time. Instead of trying to achieve what is virtually impossible—holding the target's attention for longer than 20 minutes—we need to observe the limits of the human attention span.

You're going to make the pitch in four sections or phases:

1. Introduce yourself and the big idea: 5 minutes.
2. Explain the budget and secret sauce: 10 minutes.
3. Offer the deal: 2 minutes.
4. Stack frames for a hot cognition: 3 minutes.

Phase 1: Introduce Yourself and the Big Idea

Following this formula, the very first thing you need to do—even before you think about explaining your idea—is to give people your background. But you have to do this in a specific way; your success depends on how well (and how fast) you do it. After the introductory chitchat, where you establish status and use frame control, it's natural for the target to ask, "What's your background?" or "How'd you get started in this?" At this point, you can begin the pitch, *starting with your track record of successes. Not* a long rundown of all the places you worked. *Not* all the projects you were tangentially involved with. *Not* your whole life story. The key to success here is making it about your track record. Things you built. Projects that actually worked out. Successes. Spend less than two minutes on it and definitely not more—and don't worry. Before your pitch is over, the target is going to know a whole lot more about you.

When a friend, Joe, was getting funding from Boeing, here's how he did it:

1. "My degree is from Berkeley. I did my MBA at UCLA.

2. After that I was at McKinsey for four years, but really,
   my only homerun there was the sales program I did for
   Lexus. Saved them about $15 million, and they still use it
   today.
3. I left consulting six months ago to work on the 'big idea.'"

Yes, Joe has done a lot more than that over the years, but so
what. Only his big wins are worth talking about at this point. Is
there a lot more to *your* background than this? Of course there is.
But in the pitch, time and attention are not infinite. In fact, they're
extremely scarce. And you're going to need all the time available
to get (and keep) frame control. Plan to stroke your own ego
later—when the deal is more likely to go through.

Many times I've seen people spend 15 minutes or longer on
their background. Absurd. No one is that fantastic. Yet people
often think that if some background biography is good, then
more is better. *But people's brains do not work that way.*
Research has shown that your impression of someone is generally based on the average of the available information about
them, not the sum. So telling people one great thing about yourself will leave them with a better impression of you than telling
than one great thing and one pretty good one. And it gets worse
if you tell them one great thing, one pretty good thing, and two
mediocre things. *Stop with one great thing.* Get your track record
on the table, and do it fast, clean, and problem-free. This is not
the place to get hung up with questions, deep conversations, and
analysis—*there's still a lot to do.*

Is this different from what you're used to? Is framing this way
a completely new way of looking at pitching? Yes to both. But if
you don't feel like changing to frame-based pitching, you can always
console yourself with the fact that you are not alone. Wasting time
and focusing on the wrong things are problems that exist at the
highest levels of business.

The "Why Now?" Frame

You're almost ready to pitch the "big idea." But first, a reminder of the obvious: Nobody wants to invest time or money into an old deal that has been sitting around. *This is why you need to introduce a "Why now?" frame. It's vitally important that the target knows that your idea is new, emerging from current market opportunities and that it's not some relic left over from bygone days.* The target needs to know that you are pitching a new idea that came to life from a pattern of forces that you recognized, seized, and are now taking advantage of. And the target needs to know that you have more knowledge about these things than anyone else.

There are unspoken questions in the target's mind as to why your idea is relevant and important and why it should be considered as important now. By anticipating these questions and definitively answering them before they are verbalized, you will tick an important checkbox in the target's mind and put the target more at ease. Everything you say from that point forward will have context, greater meaning, and more urgency, reinforcing its scarcity.

What I have discovered over time is that in every business there are three market forces that together triangulate to answer the "Why?" question, and you can use these forces to create a strong "Why now?" frame.

Three-Market-Forces Pattern: Trendcasting

When you describe your idea, project, or product, first give it context by framing it against these three market forces or trending patterns that you believe are important.

1. *Economic forces.* Briefly describe what has changed *financially* in the market for your big idea. For example,

are customers wealthier, is credit more available, is financial optimism higher? Increases or decreases in interest rates, inflation, and the value of the dollar are considered as prime examples of forces that have significant impact on business opportunities.

2. *Social forces.* Highlight what emerging changes in people's behavior patterns exist for your big idea. An obvious example in the market for automobiles, concern over the environment—a social force—is driving demand for electric vehicles.

3. *Technology forces.* Technological change can flatten existing business models and even entire industries because demand shifts from one product to another. In electronics, for example, change is rapid and constant, but in furniture manufacturing, change is more gradual.

Describe the genesis of your idea, how it evolved, and the opportunity you saw as it was emerging. *The backstory of the idea is always interesting to the target.* Once this story is told, everything you say in your pitch will be legitimized by it.

As you craft your backstory, think in terms of how it came to be where it is today and how you found it. Describe the steps in its evolution, and show how it evolved—how it moved—to finally become the opportunity you have now identified and captured.

The three basic steps are:

1. Explain the most important changes in our business. Forecast the trends. Identify important developments—both in your market and beyond.

2. Talk about the impact of these developments on costs and customer demand.

3. Explain how these trends have briefly opened a market window.

if you show people two pictures in rapid alternation, and one of them has some change in it—even a relatively major one—people will not see it. You can replace grandma with a tree. *It does not count as movement, and the brain ignores it.* You can hunt and hunt for what is different between the two pictures as they go back and forth and think they are identical. It is only when your attention is focused deliberately on the thing that is changing that you can finally "see" it. Once you know this fact about how your audience's mind works, *you realize that you cannot just show audience members two possible states and hope that the difference captures their attention.* You need to show them the movement from one to the other.

We are not wired to see or hear a static pitch: "*That* was the old way, but *this* is the new way." *That can trigger change blindness, where the target won't get your deal at all.* The formula I've just given you, the three changing market forces, overcomes the potential for change blindness. With three market forces coming into alignment, you are literally showing the mind's eye how the market is moving to benefit your big idea.

Here's an example of my colleague Joe giving a pitch:

"In recent years, there hasn't been much going on in the business of building new airports. In fact, it would be fair to say that the market has been dead. But now things are heating up. *Three major forces are changing the market. First,* banks have started lending to aviation projects. *Second,* the Federal Aviation Authority (FAA) is now issuing building permits. *Third,* our main competitor is excluded from bidding on this deal because of a conflict of interest."

The target sees that there's a market rationale for Joe's airport deal. *It makes sense.* The combination of the bank's new willingness to lend, the new FAA pressure on the airport, and the lack of competition have created the opportunity for this deal to happen now.

One of the most important things I've learned that has made every one of my deals possible is that targets simply do not like old deals. They want to see movement, and they don't like deals that have been sitting around, ignored by other investors or partners. It would be like the copier salesperson saying, "Hey, how would you like the Model T100? We've had 50 of them in the warehouse forever."

Introducing the Big Idea

This does not take 15 minutes. It takes 1 minute. You don't have to explain the big idea in great detail. Oh, I know you want to. It's instinctive: First, introduce yourself; then dive into details. I get the same urges. And this seems like the perfect time to do it. *But it's not time for details.* Your target doesn't want the deal yet. So the pitch temperature is cool. Lots of details will turn it cold. The details can come later. First, you will establish the big idea using an *idea introduction pattern*. The venture capitalist Geoff Moore developed this pattern in 1999, and it still works today.

The Idea Introduction Pattern

This idea introduction pattern goes like this:

> "For [target customers]
> Who are dissatstified with [the current offerings in the market].
> My idea/product is a [new idea or product category]
> That provides [key problem/solution features].
> Unlike [the competing product].
> My idea/product is [describe key features]."

Here's an example of a quick introduction for a big idea called the "EnergyTech 1000."

Example 1

"For companies with large buildings in California and Arizona
Who are dissatisfied with their aging solar panels.
My product is a plug-and-play *solar accelerator*

That provides 35 percent more energy from old panels.
And unlike the cost of replacing panels,
My product is inexpensive and has no moving parts."
That's it. The big idea can be introduced with this pattern in
about one minute.
Here's another example of the idea introduction pattern.

Example 2

"For busy executives
Who don't have enough work space on their computer monitor.
My product is a visual array
That provides eight flat-screen monitors, linked together, that
can fit on any desk.
Unlike the common do-it-yourself solutions, having just two or
three monitors,
My visual array lets executives use Excel, Firefox, Word, Gmail,
Skype, Photoshop, Explorer, and TradingDesk at the same
time with no confusing windows."
Here's how Joe used the idea introduction pattern to introduce
his airport deal.

Example 3

"For investors needing a 10 percent cash yield or better
Who are dissatisfied with risky investments such as stocks.
My airport deal is a project with low risk and lots of protection
That provides a current cash flow.
And unlike most development projects, you can cash out any
time you want."

Certainly this does a lot to capture the target's attention. *It is
important to realize, however, that capturing the target's attention*

doesn't mean that you are commanding attention. You will soon be skeptical that attention can ever be *commanded.* What's worse, you'll appreciate how it can be lost in a few seconds by making the wrong moves. The rudimentary model of how attention works goes like this: *We notice things that have movement through space and time because they are likely to be important.* But there's a catch— a lot of the time things that move are also things we have to run away from. Starting from this premise, in the pitch we want to create attention without threat. This is why I have come to believe in—and rely on—the idea introduction pattern, because, of all the ways to introduce an idea, *it does the least to trigger threat avoidance in the croc brain.*

Neuroscientist Evian Gordon is convinced that minimizing danger and threats around us is "the fundamental organizing principle of the brain." As I've said before, *the croc brain doesn't think about threats too deeply.* It just reacts. It doesn't stop to research whether the snake coming toward us is a copperhead or a cottonmouth.

Although this natural defense mechanism is beneficial in evolutionary terms, researchers believe that when we enter social situations (like a boardroom where we are expected to pitch), there's one undeniable fact—we sense a potential threat to our own well-being. For example, we could get rejected. We could embarrass ourselves. We could lose the deal or lose face. When these social threats appear, the threat-avoidance system in our own brain starts pumping adrenaline and other neurotransmitters. Anxiety kicks in. We've all felt it—that moment when we are standing in front of an audience and it feels like they're not paying attention. Our heart rate increases, our face turns flush, and sweat pores open up. We are responding to a social threat.

It's important to recognize that humans are hardwired for social interaction. So, if you haven't thought of social situations as potential threats, it's might be time to start thinking that way now.

In one study, researchers had subjects play a computer game where they thought they were throwing a digital "ball" with a few other participants. After a while of playing the game, the subject's online partners started throwing the ball *only* to each other, leaving the subject as the odd-man out. Ouch! The researchers measured the subject's reaction through brain scans. *What they found is that social threats engage the same threat-response system in the brain as physical threats do.* And to make matters worse, the brain can trigger threat responses far ahead of when you consciously become aware of the threat.

If you don't use the idea introduction pattern to deliver the big idea (or some other highly controlled way to encapsulate the big idea), here's how trouble can start brewing. First, the target picks up on your anxiety. Second, when you see the target get uncomfortable, you get more tense; you *look* tense. Third, an endless feedback loop starts: The targets senses your anxiety, and a similar threat response triggers in his system. You have lots more to do in this pitch, you've barely started, and you don't want to get caught up in a negative-feedback loop. It's too early in the pitch to start dealing with serious malfunctions.

The idea introduction pattern breaks the idea down to the essential basics: Here's what it is; here's who it's for; and here's who I compete with. No anxiety, no fear, no drama.

Let's review the actions to take in phase 1 of the pitch:

- First, you put the target at ease by telling him *in advance* that the pitch is going to be short, just about 20 minutes, and that you're not going to be hanging around too long afterward. This keeps the target's croc brain focused on the here and now and feeling safe.
- Then, you give your background in terms of a track record of successes, not a long list of places and institutions where you simply "punched the clock."

There's plenty of evidence to suggest that the more you talk about your background, the more average it becomes because the target is hardwired to average information about you, not add it up.

- Next, you show that your idea is not a static flash of genius. Rather, there are market forces driving the idea, and you are taking advantage of a brief market window that has opened. (And you've admitted that there will be competition, showing that you're not naive about business realities.)

- Because the brain pays attention to things that are in motion, you paint a picture of the idea moving out of an old market into a new one. Doing it this way, you don't trigger change blindness, which would make your deal easy to neglect.

- Last, you bring the big idea into play using the idea introduction pattern. Now the target knows exactly what it is, who it's for, who you compete with, and what your idea does better than the competition's. This simple pattern makes sure that your idea is easy to grasp and focuses on what is real. This strategy works so well because it avoids triggering a threat response.

However, this method should not imply that everything in your pitch must be simplified and reduced—you'll be delivering plenty of complex and detail-oriented information soon.

Phase 2: Explain the Budget and Secret Sauce

It's been easy to maintain the target's attention so far. In phase 1, all you had to do was introduce yourself and the big idea in about 5 minutes (or less.) In phase 2, it gets harder to hold the target's attention. Now you have to explain what problems the big idea really solves and how it actually works. *The opportunities to scare the croc brain seriously multiply when you start to explain how stuff works.*

Over the years, an enormous amount of pressure has been put on businesspeople to make their complex ideas more simple—but few gurus have come up with methods to do this that translate into real-world success. At least I haven't seen them—and I've been looking for 10 years.

The frustrating thing about simplicity is that it's *supposed* to work wonders in a presentation. Summarize your information, make it supereasy to understand, roll the concepts into an "executive summary"—the target will love you for it.

I realize that what comes next goes against conventional wisdom, but what I've discovered is that *simplicity doesn't really matter.* If it really worked, everyone would be doing it. But it doesn't, and they aren't. Simplicity can make you seem naive or unsophisticated. You can underwhelm the target with too little information just as easily as you can overwhelm him with too much information.

What you really want to do is tune the message to the mind of the target.

Think about the way you have to talk to a child. You don't just make the thing you want to say simple. For example, if you want to say, "There's no dessert being served before dinner is eaten," you don't make it *more* simple and say, "No dessert before dinner." In fact, you might have to make it even longer and more complex, explaining the reasons. Again, what's important is that a child's mind is different from your own, and you have to understand how that mind reasons. This is why it's so important to understand how the croc brain reasons. I've concluded that *ideas you come up with using your problem-solving brain—the neocortex—must be intentionally retuned for the croc brain that will receive them.*

Early in my work to figure this stuff out, I stumbled onto something cognitive psychologists called "theory of mind" that supports this. *When you have a working theory of mind, you are able to understand how thoughts, desires, and intentions of others cause them to act.* When someone can only see a situation one way, their theory of mind is weak. When you have a strong theory of mind, you recognize how other people have different perspectives—and that they know different things about the situation, and that their desires are not always the same as your desires. A strong theory of mind also will let you know that anything involving statistics needs to be highly simplified. *The croc brain hates thinking about probabilities.* Our advanced society had to invent complex formulas and equations for statistics exactly because our brains are not wired to think about statistics on their own. While there's ongoing debate about what "complexity" the average audience will like and dislike, one thing is certain: *If you're describing relationships between people, you can provide plenty of detail.* The brain is really good at understanding complex human relationships.

As I look back on my experiences, two giant realizations tower above all others:

Realization 1: It doesn't matter how much information you give, a lot or a little, but instead how good your theory of mind is. In other words, it's important how well you can tune your information to the other person's mind.

Realization 2: All the important stuff must fit into the audience's limits of attention, which for most people is about 20 minutes.

Get Their Attention

Earlier I said that one of the things that can go wrong is that your pitch is boring. In a large majority of presentations, this is the problem. In fact, virtually everyone is long-winded when they present. Yet there is absolutely no doubt among either executives or academics that audience attention fades out fast once a presentation has started. Studies of vigilance show that the targets generally can't focus on an idea for more than a few minutes. Some believe that it is a few seconds. Either way, why quibble? Attention wavers almost uncontrollably. People's minds wander. Distractions, from inside the person and the outside world, are constantly competing with your pitch. And anyway, even if there were no distractions, *the brain is still a cognitive miser—it wants to exert as little energy as possible figuring out you and your idea.*

What grabs the target's attention, and once attention is grabbed, what holds it there?

Attention will be given when information novelty is high and will drift away when information novelty is low. You already know this. If your stuff looks boring, if it has no visual stimulus, is a bunch of cold, hard facts and involves spaghetti-like complexity— no one is going to offer you much attention.

Yet there's nothing more important than attention. Oh, we can vigorously debate whether attention accounts for 70 percent of the reason someone succeeds with a pitch or 50 percent, but no one can seriously question that getting and holding attention are the biggest reasons a pitch either connects with the target and succeeds or misses the target and fails.

Looking at it another way, if the target were willing to pay attention to you for a few hours, then just about any pitch—good or bad—would work. *But you don't have hours.* More likely, you've got those 20 minutes we've been talking about. And maybe, if you're just winging it, you only have five minutes before your pitch wanders into a mental no-man's land.

What Is Attention?

To control attention, I have always felt that it's important to know what it's made of. Attention is a sort of vague, all-encompassing term that seems to just *define itself.* But who would ever try to make a martini without knowing what's in it first? I phrase the question this way because you'll see in a moment that attention is just that—a cocktail of chemicals served up to the brain as a lubricant for social interaction. You need to know how to blend this perfect cocktail and when to serve it.

How did I find what the ingredients are? I didn't have to. Researchers with brain scanners and hardcore neuroscience chops did the work. What they've worked out is that *when a person is feeling both desire and tension, that person is paying serious attention to what's in front of him or her.*

The critical lesson of brain scans is that attention is always a delicate and unstable balancing act between desire and tension. It comes down to the presence of two neurotransmitters: dopamine and norepinephrine.

> *Dopamine* is the neurotransmitter of *desire.*
> *Norepinephrine* is the neurotransmitter of *tension.*
> Together they add up to *attention.*

If you want someone's undivided, fully engaged attention, you have to provide these two neurotransmitters. These two chemicals work together—you need them both to be coursing through the crocodile brain of the target. But each has a different triggering mechanism.

To give a dopamine kick and create desire, *offer a reward.*

To give a norepinephrine kick and create tension, *take something away.*

You're going to learn the patterns for triggering the desire and tension right now.

What Does Dopamine Do?   Dopamine is the chemical in the brain that chases rewards. It takes about 1/20 of a second for dopamine to guide humans toward some kind of action. Dopamine levels rise in the brain when you see or hear about something you want. When you see a person acting curious, open-minded, and interested in something—it's dopamine that's motivating them. A strong cup of coffee, Yohimbe root, cocaine, and the cold medication sudafed all increase dopamine levels in the brain. In most people, so does the thought of winning a large gamble or of even buying what's known as an *ornament*—like a Rolex watch or some other status-enhancing product.

Dopamine release in the brain is connected to *pleasure activities*, such things as food, sex, and drugs. But now brain scans show that dopamine isn't exactly the chemical of experiencing pleasure. Instead, it's the chemical of *anticipating a reward.* In his book, *Satisfaction*, Dr. Greg Berns explains this: "How do you get more dopamine flowing in your brain? NOVELTY. A raft of brain imaging experiments has demonstrated that novel events ... are highly effective at releasing dopamine. Your brain is stimulated by surprise because our world is fundamentally unpredictable." He adds, "You may not always like novelty, but your brain does."

You create novelty by violating the target's expectations in a pleasing way.

Let's review. When you introduce something novel to the target's brain, a release of dopamine occurs. This triggers desire. For example:

A short product demo provides novelty.

A new idea provides novelty.

Good metaphors for otherwise complex subjects provide
    novelty.

Bright objects, moving objects, and unique shapes, sizes, and
    configurations all provide novelty.

You want the audience's full attention, and you want to erase everything else audience members are paying attention to, so introduce
novelty.

How Dopamine Leads the Feeling of Novelty.   Until now, I've
talked about the raw amount of information that comes into the
brain and how it all can't be processed at once. All this information
and data from the senses collect in one small part of the brain.
There has to be some way of selecting what to ignore and what to
act on. Dopamine motivates the human body to act on some things
and ignore others.

Research done at the University College London, written about
by *Wall Street Journal* reporter Jason Zweig, suggests that getting
what you expected to get produces no dopamine kick, but a novelty in the form of an unexpected gain gives the brain a blast of
dopamine. On the other hand, if a reward you expected fails to
materialize, then dopamine dries up, and negative feelings start
happening.

Just like the martini making we talked about earlier, the
amount of dopamine in the cocktail has to be just right. *Not
enough, and there is no interest in your or your ideas; too much,
and there is fear or anxiety.*

Earlier we also talked about the importance of a simple introduction to your big idea but that simple is not always better. The
dopamine kick explains why: *People enjoy some intermediate level*

of intellectual complexity. It has been argued that people are curious about things they cannot explain but that seem explainable—mystery stories work this way. And this, of course, is why novelty is so important in the pitch. Curiosity is the croc brain becoming interested—feeling like it's safe to learn more. Curiosity derives from an information gap—the difference between what you know and what you want to know. This is the addictive quality of curiosity—and what you are trying to create for the target: curiosity about the big idea.

It's only when the target feels that he knows enough to fully understand your big idea that the curiosity ends—and he becomes satiated. *At that point of satiation, whether you recognize it or not, the pitch is over.*

Novel information has the potential to trigger one of two responses—retreat or exploration. Curiosity is a feeling of novel information taking on the second, exploratory path, which is the first step toward a satisfying intellectual experience.

When a signal from the pitch tells the target there is something new to be discovered, dopamine is released in the brain. Unexpected (and pleasant) rewards release more dopamine than expected ones. But dopamine has a dark side, too; if the target is expecting a reward and don't get it, dopamine levels fall off fast. And when dopamine levels drop that fast, the feeling of stress is just around the corner. Not only does the target stop taking in new information from you, but he starts forgetting the information you've already delivered.

In summary, expecting rewards generates dopamine. Dopamine is the buzz of novelty. Alone, however, it's not enough to create attention. While dopamine is the chemical of curiosity, interest, and desire, it can't generate attention without norepinephrine, which tends to create tension, and this is why I call it the *chemical of alertness.*

Tension

In the earlier discussion of novelty and desire, I talked about just half the formula for creating attention. The other half of that formula is *tension*. First, let's start with some definitions: *Tension* is the introduction of some real consequences to the social encounter. It's the response to a clear and unequivocal realization that something will be gained or lost. It is letting the target know that there are high stakes. *Tension indicates consequences and therefore importance.*

There's no reason for the target to pay attention when there are no stakes—when tension is absent. A few words about the purpose of tension will help. Here we are interested in the interplay between pushing the target away and pulling him toward us. Not as a point of manipulation—at no point in the pitch are we ever interested in that—but as a way to keep the target alert. If you want your target focused and energized—to really pay full attention—you also must get him to stay alert. Tension accomplishes this by injecting a shot of norepinephrine into the target's brain.

This brings us to an examination of the relationship between novelty and tension. Without both, Dennis, the avocado farmer, loses $640,000; *Jaws* becomes one of the worst movies of all time; and Benoit, the French waiter, can barely make a living.

We may never have thought about attention this way before, as a cocktail of neurotransmitters, and honestly, why bother now? We certainly don't know what neurotransmitters are, and if we're being honest with ourselves, this is something we don't really care about at a deep level. To most of us, it's worthwhile only in that it illustrates the following:

> *The two parts of the attention cocktail are novelty and tension, which in a pitch work together in a feedback loop for about 20 minutes until—no matter what you do or how hard you try—they get out of balance and then stop working altogether.*

Tension comes from conflict. Some beginning presenters want to rely on their charisma (a pure form of novelty) and try to avoid all conflict in their pitch narrative. They want everyone to play nice. Only smiles, no grimaces. Why? Because in regular life, outside the pitch, confrontation can be stressful and nerve wracking, so it makes sense that we would try to avoid it everywhere. *But in narrative- and frame-based pitching, you can't be afraid of tension. In fact, you have to create it.*

The rudimentary patterns I have outlined below have proved extremely rewarding in my career. This might seem surprising—and not because patterns are so simple and basic, but because they are intended to build tension. This is what has given me an edge.

There are three tension patterns, each with an increasing level of intensity. These are conversational patterns you can use at any point in a presentation when you sense the target's attention dropping.

Low-Key, Low-Intensity Push/Pull Pattern.

PUSH: "There's a real possibility that we might not be right for each other."

[Pause. Allow the push to sink in. It must be authentic.]

PULL: "But then again, if this did work out, our forces could combine to become something great."

Medium-Intensity Push/Pull Pattern.

PUSH: "There's so much more to a deal than just the idea.
I mean, there's a venture-capital group in San Francisco that
doesn't even care what the idea is—they don't even look at it
when a deal comes in. The only thing they care about is *who*
the people are behind the deal. That makes sense. I've learned
that ideas are common, a dime a dozen. What really counts is
having someone in charge who has passion and experience
and integrity. So if you and I don't have that view in common,
it would never work between us."
[Pause.]
PULL: "But that's crazy to think. *Obviously* you value people
over smart ideas. I've met corporate robots before that only
care about numbers—and you are definitely not a robot."

High-Intensity Push/Pull Pattern.

PUSH: "Based on the couple of reactions I'm getting from you—*it
seems like this isn't a good fit.* I think that you should only do
deals where there is trust and deals you strongly believe in. So
let's just wrap this up for now and agree to get together on the
next one."
*[Pause. Wait for a response. Start packing up your stuff. Be
willing to leave if the target doesn't stop you.]*

*There's a two-way connection between pushing and pulling
that, when it operates simultaneously, introduces enough tension
to create alertness.* If you always pull the target toward you, he or
she becomes cautious and anxious. Constantly pulling someone in,
also known as *selling hard*, is a signal of neediness. It's a balancing act, of course, because if you are constantly pushing them away,
they will take the hint and leave.

One of the most celebrated examples of this push/pull in the Pitch community involves *Mad Men*'s Don Draper, a pitchman for a fictional ad agency who gets a negative reaction from a client during a pitch. He pushes.

"Looks like there's not much else to do here. Let's call it a day," he tells the client, extending a handshake. "Gentlemen, thank you for your time." *Draper stands up to leave.*

I've watched the clip on many occasions, and the result always leaves me with a greater appreciation for the perfect push/pull delivery, one that creates a blast of norepinephrine in the client's brain.

In the clip, the tension grows as the client, surprised, asks, "Is that all?"

Draper replies, "You're a nonbeliever. Why should we waste time on Kabuki [theater]?"

The client responds to the push—suddenly interested in Draper's ideas and paying attention, he asks Draper to sit back down.

Perhaps the most outstanding example of a push/pull pattern that I've encountered occurred some years ago when an audience tried to impose its will on me at a conference.

I was offered an opportunity to pitch my deals to a handful of the most influential investors in a $10 billion market. How could I resist? I would meet them at an upcoming conference in a closed-room, one-on-one experience. The conference organizers charged me $18,000 for the privilege, and they set it all up.

I gladly paid the fee, and I jumped my company jet to Denver, looking forward to a great opportunity to generate new business. After breakfast, I went up to the conference room, ready to rock. I walked in and was shocked by what I saw.

Inside the room were 25 people—more than I expected—and here was the kicker: They were not investors or buyers. They were *due-diligence analysts*. I shook my head. I couldn't believe it.

A *due-diligence analyst*, as the name suggests, is someone whose job is to analyze and evaluate a deal based on facts and figures. These are neocortex people, and they are tough to pitch because they are all about numbers and are trained to avoid emotion. Imagine a bunch of nicely dressed robots looking for flaws in everything you do and say. Dealing with just one of these people is hard enough, but now I stood in front of 25 of them. And none of them could pull the trigger on a deal, anyhow. This was the worst possible audience for my deal.

The tables and chairs were set up in a U-shape, and I stepped up in the horseshoe, despite my misgivings. I started my pitch by passing out our marketing materials—a beautiful 56-page deal book.

The book outlined the math behind a new kind of financial technique called *bifurcation*, which can really amplify profits. As the audience studied it page by page, I launched into my pitch. And I absolutely nailed it—or so I thought. But my pitch was all dopamine and no epinephrine—that is to say, *all promise of reward and no tension*. I looked up at one point, hoping to see smiling faces, expecting to hear a barrage of questions from these due-diligence guys. Instead, I got stone cold faces looking back at me. Silence. Not a single question. Imagine looking out at 25 concrete garden gnomes. I can't remember such a nonresponse to one of my pitches. Ever! This doesn't mean that the targets were unreachable. It just means that they had strong analyst frames that were not easily disrupted.

I said, "Guys, since you can't think of any questions to throw at me, let me get those bifurcation books back from you." I started walking around the horseshoe, taking them gently out of their hands. In some cases, I had to pull more aggressively. That's when I knew: *I had the prize frame.* Now they had something to lose—and questions started flowing. Over the next two years, I closed over $5 million with these targets.

To hold your target's attention, there must be tension—a form of low-level conflict—guiding the interaction. If there's no conflict, the target may be politely "listening," but there's no real connection. The target is thinking, "He seems like a nice guy, and his idea seems good, but I have other things to worry about right now."

This is a confidence problem. I used to be afraid of creating tension. I was afraid to do anything that might upset the target in any way. Sure, when you and the target are each nodding in happy agreement, it *feels* great in the moment. You think to yourself, *it's a lovefest.* But when it goes on too long with no counterbalance— it's boring. At the end, the target gets up and says, "That was really nice," and then walk away. Targets want a challenge of some sort. They don't want the easy answers.

If there's a single reason why some of my most important pitches failed, it's because I was nice and the audience was nice, and we were all very polite with each other. There was no tension or conflict. Conflict is the basis of interesting human connections.

As businesspeople, we come together to find solutions to problems—not to admire problems that have already been solved for us. If you don't have a series of challenges for the target to overcome—with pushes and pulls and tension loops—then you don't have a *pitch narrative.*

A pitch narrative can be thought of as a series of tension loops. Push then pull. Create tension. Then resolve it.

When there's no tension between you and the target, there's no interest in what happens. The target also has no emotional involvement in what's going on. In other words, the target doesn't much care about what you do, why you're doing it, or what happens to you after you leave. Without tension loops, nothing is compelling the reader to stay with the pitch storyline.

The Heart of the Pitch

Once you have attention by creating desire and tension—you're ready to deliver the heart of your pitch. But keep moving fast because this cocktail of dopamine and norepinephrine you're serving is sloshing around in the brain of the target in the right combination for just a few minutes. And as we discussed earlier, no matter how hard you work, eventually the target's desire is going to become fear, and the tension in the room is going to turn into anxiety.

The greatest problem in short-form pitching is deciding what details and specifics to single out for attention—what to leave in and what to leave out. And since I'll need to give you specific examples, I think that selling a company or raising money is a good framework in which to discuss this subject. For one thing, it is the market with which I am most familiar. I have been working in the capital markets for about 15 years. For another, these markets have provided a fantastic test bed for me because hard data and fast feedback have been readily available. I've got this down to a method.

Actually delivering the core of the pitch is very straightforward stuff. The main requirement is that you understand that what's happening in your mind is not what's happening in the target's mind. Package the information for the croc brain, as I described in Chapter 1. Big picture. High contrast. Visual. Novel. With verified evidence.

Before you decide to spend too much time on this part of the presentation, remember that the following items are a simple punchlist of issues that most pitches have to cover. *These are the prerequisites.* The stuff you *have* to have no matter what. It's the minimum information you need to show up and be relevant.

Recognize that you can be incredible at turning a business plan into an executive summary or any other kind of elevator pitch and still have that pitch fail miserably. Doing a good job here is not about some genius new way of organizing and presenting information. Would you argue? We don't need yet another organizing theory for information. The basics work fine. What we need is a way to present this material without the target becoming too analytical about it.

When it comes to a choice of what to focus on when pitching the plan that will make the big idea work, I would start by presenting the budget because most people screw this up. It's your chance to be different.

Pitching Numbers and Projections

In his book *High Tech Ventures*, Gordon Bell writes, "Start-ups often prepare absurdly aggressive and optimistic plans, which have a very low likelihood of success, just to maximize the company's perceived dollar value." Your financial projections, whether for a product or a company, are supposed to answer such basic questions as, How strong is the company? What if plans go awry, does the company have enough cash to last a few bad quarters? Do you know how to budget well?

A word of caution, however, as you approach these topics: Every experienced buyer and investor knows that you will be doing these two things:

1. Saying that your budgets are "conservative"
2. Preparing *absurdly aggressive and optimistic plans*

To the investor, for example, every pro forma looks the same, a hockey stick chart that shows the following: *We need lots of money today, and way down the road we'll make it back* (sometimes it works out that way; usually it doesn't).

Unrealistic budgets and miscalculating costs are the greatest risks to a growing company, especially startups. How do you get around the skepticism that surely will fall on your plans? *Focus on demonstrating your skill at budgeting, which is a difficult and highly regarded executive talent.* Spend almost no time on your skills at projecting revenue—a task any simpleton can perform.

Competition

The act of introducing the budgets to the target will lead him or her to wonder, Who does the big idea compete with? This is a valid question that you cannot ignore. The attractiveness of an idea is based on the industry it's in and how much competition there is. Yet almost no one describes the competition they face in adequate terms. Let's do it right in the pitch. Here are the two major elements of competition:

1. How easy it is for new competitors to jump in the game?
2. How easy it is for customers to switch out your product with another?

Secret Sauce

To avoid the impression that you are a come-and-go idea that will shine brightly in the market one day and be forgotten soon after, you'll need to show what your competitive advantage is based on. This one thing will give you staying power against competition. In almost every pitch situation, you need something special. Briefly describe it as your "secret sauce"—the *unfair advantage* you have over others.

You don't have to get too fancy here—just don't take longer than 10 minutes to describe the fundamental workings of your big idea—because you're going to need the last five minutes to offer the deal and stack the frames.

Think the need to move fast doesn't apply to you? *You want to leisurely take an hour to do all this?* I've met many people who don't believe in the limits of human attention and feel exempt from the consequences of running long. An investment banker I know brags, "I can read them the phone book for an hour, and they'll pay attention." Is the science wrong—should we forget about dopamine and epinephrine cocktails entirely?

Consider for a minute the actor Jerry Seinfeld. His movie, *Comedian*, is a behind-the-scenes look at the business of performing comedy. In it, Seinfeld reveals the difficulty of being in front of an audience. He is one of the most recognized personalities anywhere in the world. Probably the best-known comedian on the planet. Sure, there's Chris Rock, Dave Chappelle, and Robin Williams, but really, when you think about it, Jerry Seinfeld is as big as it gets.

When he decides to go on the road to test new material, Jerry says that it's not as easy as you might think. He can walk on the stage anywhere, even a small town, and it's clear that the audience knows he's one of the most accomplished performers of modern times, with over $1 billion of television revenues. They're thrilled to be in the presence of a man so popular and funny. *But the thrill doesn't last long.*

"I have about three minutes where they will just listen to whatever I have to say," Seinfeld says. "But after that—it can fall apart fast. I get no credit. After three minutes, I have to be just as funny as any other comedian. That's it—three minutes."

And there's more to the story. Seinfeld became aware of the three-minute mark because it takes him as long as a month of full-time work to build up just three minutes of quality content. When he first goes out on tour, that's about all the material he starts with. Three minutes. It takes him months more of steady work to build up 20 minutes of material that can hold an audience's attention. That's worth thinking about. One of the most well-known performers and presenters in the world has to put in months of hard work to build up 20 minutes of material—and when he eventually goes on stage, the average audience will cut him slack for only three minutes. After that, the material had better be really good, or the audience will turn on him.

So when we frame the issue of how long a pitch should be, with the Jerry Seinfeld story in mind, it becomes easier to understand why time is so precious in the pitch: How long can you really be interesting to listen to? Perhaps there is someone who can pitch a deal as dull as the phone book for an hour, which is up to three times the basic limits of human attention, but if so, he or she is a lot smarter and more charismatic than Seinfeld or any other entertainer.

Phase 3: Offer the Deal

In the third phase of the Pitch process, you need to do one thing and do it well: Describe to your audience what they are going to receive when they decide to do business with you. You'll want to push through this quickly for the sake of time—and get back to framing.

In clear and concise terms, tell the audience exactly what you will be delivering to them, when it will be delivered, and how. If they play a part in this process, explain what their roles and responsibilities will be. Don't drill down into a lot of detail; just provide summarized facts that they need to know so that their mental picture of your offering is complete.

It does not matter if you are offering a product, a service, an investment, or an intangible—there will be a fulfillment process involved, and that is what you must explain.

Keep it brief but rich in high-level details so there is no question as to what the audience is going to get. And remember, the most important deliverable in your deal is you.

Chapter 5

Frame Stacking and Hot Cognitions

In Chapter 4, I showed you the first three phases of a pitch. By this point, you have held the target's attention for a while. The target knows the essentials: who you are, why this idea is important, how it works, what the "secret sauce" is—and what the target gets when he or she buys. But you're here to do more than just show and tell; this is a pitch, and you're here to make a deal happen. Now you have about five minutes left to propose something concrete and actionable—something so compelling that it will cause your target to chase you to get what you have.

Welcome to the next phase.

Phase 4: Frame Stacking and Hot Cognitions

In the course of my activities seeking out money for deals, I discovered that investors do not operate only on cold, rational calculation. Do you think that the guy sitting across the table from you is an analytical machine?

> The target can like your deal (or be afraid of it) before he knows much detail about it—and the target probably can decide "Yes" or "No" without even knowing what it is. This is *hot cognition* at work. *Deciding that you like something before you fully understand it—that's a hot cognition.*

We have been led to believe over time by managers, consultants, bankers, and professors of finance that business is analytical. That it's rational. That there are three very well-ordered stages in each business decision: Identify the problem, examine solutions, and make judgments. This makes sense, and this is how it should be in a perfect economic world. In fact, if you took out a blank sheet of paper and asked yourself, "How *should* I make this decision?" that's how you probably *would* do it. Research. Analyze. Decide. And if we were all computer-like or even behaved like rational economists think we do, it *would* work this way. But we aren't, and it doesn't. What's intriguing here is that when we decide on something, we believe that it's because we really "thought it through" or we "used a decision matrix." We think that we are smart, careful, and rational decision makers.

In decision making, however, we don't do much analysis, if any at all. We go with our gut. When Jack Welch eventually wrote his biography, it wasn't called *Intense Analysis*; it was titled, *Straight from the Gut*. And when George Soros updates his next edition of *The Alchemy of Finance*, he's going to include the research of Dr. Flavia Cymbalista, who believes that we feel decisions in our body, not our mind.

There's a whole side to us that computers don't have and the "rational economic man" economists like to talk about doesn't have either. Our bodies "know" the situations we meet in life and how we should respond.

"Brain Scanners Can See Your Decisions Before You Make Them" is the title of a provocative article that appeared in *Wired*. The first line in the article reads, "You may think you decided to read this story—but in fact, your brain made the decision long before you knew about it," referring to a study by John-Dylan Haynes, a Max Planck Institute neuroscientist. Haynes says, "Your decisions are strongly prepared by brain activity. By the time consciousness kicks in, most of the work has already been done."

The patterns he found in the brain consistently predicted whether test subjects eventually pushed a button with their left or right hand—about seven seconds before they felt they had made a conscious choice to do it. Do you still think that your decisions are postconscious, in other words, that you rationally think about things and make decisions afterwards? The peer group is shrinking of people who think like that.

We Tend to Like (or Dislike) Things Before We Know Much About Them

People do not become friends with each other, choose one career over another, or choose what sport to watch on the weekend based on a detailed cognitive analysis of the pros and cons of each situation. If we stop to think about it, most major decisions are *not* made by cold cognitive processes such as evaluation and analysis but instead by *hot cognition*. We quickly realize that there probably are very few decisions in our lives that aren't "hot."

Most of the time, the data we have collected about choices and alternatives and options aren't used to make a decision anyway. They are used *to justify decisions after the fact*. We buy the cars we "like," choose the jobs and houses that we find "attractive," and then justify those choices to other people with any number of facts and explanations. "Why this deal?" or "Why this investment?" We don't need facts and explanations to convince ourselves. We know what we like. *Even when we try the rational approach—making lists of pros and cons—if it does not come out how we like, we go back and redo the list until it does.*

If you had invested $1,000 with George Soros when he opened his Quantum Fund, you would have about $4 million today. Yet he is known for whimsically changing his investment tactics— we're talking market positions of hundreds of millions of dollars— on a feeling in his back or some other physical signal.

Cymbalista, who has studied Soros and financial decision making, writes, "This might sound mysterious but, in fact, human thinking is constantly guided by subtle bodily tensions. Traders need to learn how to isolate and identify these bodily tensions and relate them to the analysis of the market problem at hand. Certainly, Soros has learned how to combine theory and instinct to make money."

George Soros' backache decision-making is consistent with the research of Dr. Jerome Bruner. According to Bruner, "There are two modes of cognitive functioning, two modes of thought, each providing distinctive ways of ordering experience and constructing reality." Bruner says that one mode of "constructing reality" is called the *paradigmatic mode* (one can think of this as the detective mode). In paradigmatic mode, the target takes the content of your pitch and analyzes it in terms of "tightly reasoned analysis, logical proof and empirical observation." In other words, the information you're providing is getting analyzed. If you push your listener into this mode, he or she is looking to find a formula that explains you. *Your audience/target will be doing only one thing in paradigmatic mode—trying to analyze. All your creative concepts, future projections, and human inferences are going to be ignored by the analytical/paradigmatic thinker. The only thing that will count are cold, hard facts.*

In our pitch, we are *not* looking to engage with the cold neocortex. We are *not* going to push the target into paradigmatic mode. And we don't need a quantitative analysis of our numbers done by the target right now. Sure, our numbers will stand up to scrutiny and we're not afraid of a stress test—but there will be a time for cold analysis later once the relationship is firmly set in place.

Creating Hot Cognition

To avoid cold, reasoned analysis, unemotional judgment of ourselves and our idea, *we are going to create hot cognition by stacking frames.* I came to learn about stacking frames by accident.

How to Stack Frames

Part of my work involves buying "defaulted debt" with a partner—specifically high-risk debt. It's a hard-knocks game where it seems that you either do very well or you get *crushed.* My partner did about $250 million in transactions from 2008 through 2010. In this field, however, $250 million is small time among the multibil-lion-dollar hedge funds and the giants of Wall Street with whom we work—Citi, Goldman Sachs, JP Morgan. Our success is based on keeping alert and making quick, small trades of $20 million to $50 million. We are like gazelles running among elephants. In this game, if you sense a giant foot coming down, you take off running because if JP Morgan, Chase Manhattan, or Goldman Sachs steps on you, they wouldn't even notice. But you would.

In June 2008, the market was in the early stages of a scream-ing freefall that bottomed out in March 2009. And we knew it was bad, but we didn't know how bad it was going to get: At one point, the housing market in Phoenix dropped 9 percent in a single month. Movements of the Dow Jones Industrial Index of 100 points a day was the norm. Any Wall Street trader knows that you want to be careful trading in this kind of volatility because a sin-gle mistake can cause you to blow up.

Buying distressed assets sounds like it should be easy. After all, the market was crumbling and everyone needed to sell their toxic assets.

At the time, I was doing a deal with a trading desk at one of the largest money-center banks. I needed another point of view on the deal, so I called a colleague, Mike. He had a lot of experience in this kind of deal—and a second opinion is always good. I thought that the price was high, and I wasn't sure about the deal.

Now, as I stayed late at work on a Wednesday night, the phone rang. It was a trader at this large money-center Wall Street bank, and this was his fifth call to me. In the back of my croc brain, threat alerts started going off. Why was this $300 billion bank courting me so hard? There had to be better buyers than me in the market? But once I started talking to the trader, I realized that he wasn't selling me in the traditional ways.

From the beginning, I never felt like he was selling me. My normal deal-making processes were disrupted by this four-frame stack. The Wall Street trader ran this stack on me *perfectly*: I was intrigued, I was trying to impress him so I could have a chance to buy the deal, he boxed me into a very tight time frame and yet I felt no pressure, and I was trying hard to prove that I had a good moral values. I was a puppet. My cold analytical decision processes weren't just disrupted; they were shut down and turned off. My neocortex was short-circuited, and my croc brain was rolling around in cognitive mud, happy and calm. I was going to do the deal. And the next day I called the Wall Street trader back and said, "Send me the docs. I'm doing it!"

There's no question that the pitch worked on me. Fortunately, it also worked on Mike.

Mike Hanson soon called me, bragging that he had taken down the deal—*stolen it right out of my eager hands*. Thank God for that. Two years later, he was still down 15 percent in that trade and losing money daily. He was miserable with the deal. For me, though, it had worked out fine.

I had learned the *four-frame hot cognition stack*.

Now, a few years later, I've found that this stack works in many kinds of pitches. And it's a lot of fun for both me and the targets. It's hot, emotional, and fast-paced. When the target starts getting analytical and cold, it's time for the four-frame hot cognition stack to enter the pitch.

To make it work, you just implement the frames you are already familiar with from Chapter 2. All you have to do is learn how to stack them up one after the other to generate a *hot cognition*—in other words, to create what cognitive scientists call a *wanting*.

Specifically, we're *not* trying to get the target to "like" us because learning to "like" something is the slow and intellectual

"Oren, once we get through this deal, and we know you close deals, I'm going to introduce you to our senior trader, J Kincaid," the seller told me. "He's a wildman, just like you. going to be a total love connection, and he'll get you into the deals that don't come to my desk."

This was *hot cognition 1*—intrigue. I wanted to meet the se trader and get introduced to these bigger deals.

The bank trader continued: "You know the market is on right now, and I have the French, English, and South Africans ging me for this package, but if you work hard and don't play funny retrade games, you can earn your way in." It was true market was hot, and those were all players.

This was *hot cognition 2*—prizing. Although I was the b he was asking me to prove myself. I wanted to impress him so I could earn my way into the deal.

He continued: "I'd love to give you until next week, but market is not letting me, and you have to make up your min Friday." He said, "I'm totally okay with a 'No'; there's no sure. But Friday is D-day."

This was *hot cognition 3*—time frame. He gave me just en time that I felt I had free will. This wasn't time pressure, just a sonable time constraint. In the end, the decision was mine to n

He continued: "And I don't need to tell you, we've done $15 lion in trades this year without a single SEC [Securities and Excl Commission] sanction; right now we're very particular about ou utation and counterparties. We do things right over here, so no g no missing wire numbers, just clean paper. We give you a fair and that's the deal. Can you play by the rules?"

This was *hot cognition 4*—moral authority. I assured hin even though my company was small, just a $250 million blip c outskirts of San Diego, I knew the rules and could do things business of the neocortex. This is not the business we're in. We want high-temperature frames that create hot cognitions. And we're using frame stacks to make sure that the target's croc brain wants us and moves toward us—even ends up chasing us to get the deal. Let's do it now.

Here are the four frames we're going to stack in quick succession. (Doing this correctly will move you quickly into the last part of the pitch—the *hookpoint*.)

Hot cognition 1: the intrigue frame.
Hot cognition 2: the prize frame.
Hot cognition 3: the time frame.
Hot cognition 4: the moral authority frame.

Hot Cognition 1: The Intrigue Frame

In Chapter 2, we talked about the theory of *frame-based pitching*, and I introduced the *intrigue frame. Now we're going to use it.* The purpose is to get a large dopamine dump into the croc brain of the target—and build desire. I do this by introducing something the target is sure to want—but cannot get right now.

Here's the intrigue frame I used recently in a situation where I had given the pitch, offered up the deal, but, before I could blink, was getting hammered with technical questions:

"Guys, before we spend our last few minutes on financial details, let's decide first if you love me and you love the basic deal. And look, if you decide that you do love the deal, you're obviously going to meet my partner Joshua," I tell them. "He's a very interesting guy, a great guy, but a little eccentric."

I see if I have their attention, which I usually do. People like to hear stories about interesting and slightly eccentric characters.

"Last year, when the markets were volatile, I had this little deal, about $10 million," I tell them. "It seemed easy because it was such a small deal, and I was the only one working it. Things were going like clockwork until the bank called and at the eleventh hour and backed out. No explanation; they just pulled out. That left a $3 million hole in the plan—the deal was falling apart fast. This had come out of the blue, and I was sure that the board of directors of my company would fire me when they found out about the screw-up. I knew I had to go to Joshua with this."

My audience leans in. They want to find out how the problem was solved. And who is this Joshua? They are intrigued.

"Joshua asked me, 'Oren, is this a good deal?' I said, 'Yes, it's good. Let me tell you all about it." But he didn't stick around to listen. Instead, he went to lunch, without even giving me time to grovel. What could I do? I had to save the investors—and myself too. I wanted to pitch Joshua, to do anything to convince him to save the deal. He, it seemed, just wanted to eat lunch. I was preparing for my funeral when I got the call from the board. They had mysteriously gotten the $3 million. Joshua had wired it in, from his BlackBerry, while having sushi. He didn't ask me to sign any guarantees. He didn't even ask to see the file. If he hadn't made that wire, my investors would have lost a lot of money, and my reputation would have taken a hit. The thing about it is that he does this kind of stuff all the time. Wait until you meet him!"

This is the kind of narrative that targets truly enjoy. Who is this mystery man, Joshua, and how do we meet him? This works because it is not about *what* happened. That's actually a boring story. What's important is *who it happened to and how the characters reacted to their situation.* Nobody cares about narratives where you witnessed something. They want to see someone forced into action and positively overcoming obstacles. This new notion of building an intrigue frame makes a lot of sense when you think about *why* the target is sitting there listening to *your* pitch.

The targets have given you their time because they want to visit a new world to learn about new things and interesting ideas and become involved in the lives of unique, interesting, and talented people.

No one is seriously going to go into business with you until they know something about how you conduct yourself in tough situations. And it's no use telling anyone, "I'm a good person." That's a useless analytical fact that has no narrative to support it.

People want to know how you have faced obstacles and overcome them. They want to see you in situations that reveal your character. They want to know that you are someone who rises to whatever level necessary to overcome obstacles and someone who travels in the company of interesting people who are players in whatever game you are playing.

This kind of story, according to Dr. Bruner, puts the target into narrative thinking mode. In narrative mode, we seek to understand reality from events in terms of "human actors striving to do physical things over time." And from this simple statement, we draw an important insight: Your big idea is probably an abstract notion. If you are honest with yourself, what is it *really*? A pile of financials, a bunch of timelines, some customer orders, a marketing plan, an Internet site, and some smart new ideas. You probably have projections, information technology, competitive analysis, and market timing. This kind of info is much too abstract.

The target's brain does not love abstract concepts—every abstract concept has to be kicked up to the neocortex to be worked on, slowly and painstakingly.

This is why you need analog human narratives to do your explaining. They don't have to be sent to the neocortex for processing. For example, the Joshua story is anchored in the real world with human characters: The target can relate to the human elements in it.

Why is the intrigue frame best performed as a narrative? Here's how the target's brain interprets narratives at the crocodile level:

In narrative mode, the croc brain sees human characters confronting real-world obstacles in time scales that make sense. The croc brain can sort of verify events in time because they are easy to relate to our previous experiences and understanding of how the world works. If the unfolding of events, as told by you, feels accurate to the target, then a truth is assigned to it. *A narrative that feels correct in time will convey a strong sense of truth and accuracy.*

In stark contrast, facts and figures have no built-in internal mechanism for feeling the truth. If we present just facts and figures, then we trigger a paradigmatic mode that encourages the target to use logical rigor over imagination, intellect over feeling, and theories over stories. Clearly, you don't want your target in this paradigmatic thinking. *Short and strong narratives that introduce characters who are overcoming real-world obstacles can ignite hot cognitions—which, in turn, push the target out of paradigmatic and analytical thinking mode.*

There's a basic formula for developing this kind of intrigue frame.

Narrative Pattern for Building an Intrigue Frame. Intrigue frames, like all narratives, whether fiction or nonfiction, need structure. Without structure, a story wanders around without purpose and becomes boring. Here's a pattern that will give any of your stories a dramatic arc that ends with intrigue:

- Put a man in the jungle.

- Have beasts attack him.
- Will he get to safety?

Clearly, being stuck in the jungle is a metaphor for being in a difficult situation. The attacking beasts are the conflict and tension. These are the problems being faced by the man and the motivation for him to start moving toward safety. Once he is out of the jungle, the tension is resolved and the narrative arc is complete, so hold the man just short of safety as long as you want to use the intrigue frame.

This is going to give you a narrative arc that takes the target, quickly, on a strong emotional ride that has conflict and tension, and doing it this way will fire the hot cognition.

Things don't always need to be told in terms of extreme events—but they always should be extreme in terms of the character's emotional experience. This is what makes a good narrative.

Why use this pattern? The man-in-the-jungle formula forces you to deliver a narrative in a human, active way where you do something in the real world that shows drive and tenacity, self-confidence, and a connection to reality.

When we listen to your narrative, it's not what happens to you that makes you interesting, but it's what you do about the situations you are in. The emotional power in a narrative comes from a character that engages difficult obstacles and finds ways to overcome them.

Here's another example of the pattern, where I built an intrigue frame with a compelling narrative. I was taught this pattern by a Hollywood screenwriter. It's called the "ticking time bomb":

Put a man in the jungle. I had an $18 million deal some time ago in which I was responsible for finding $6.4 million from investors (the bank would provide the rest of the money).

It took about 10 days, and I had commitments on for all $6.4 million. Then, less than 72 hours before closing, something unwanted happened.

The beasts attack. One of the investors, Jeff Jacobs, went AWOL. His bank would not wire the money without his signature, and I could not close the deal. That was a Friday afternoon. The entire $18 million deal was in jeopardy. I was imagining the worst: Maybe he was at the bottom of his Malibu swimming pool clutching a bag of bricks and a "goodbye cruel world" note. I spent all weekend looking for him—but he could not be found. By Monday morning, I had less than eight hours to come up with either Jeff Jacobs or his money. All my phones were ringing. On the other end of the line: the other investors, the bank, the seller, and my partners. Each caller was madder than the last.

Will he get out of the jungle? I sat down at the computer and started e-mailing consultants and sales types in our industry. I offered $1,000 for any kind of information on Jacobs. One of them found me a second address and a phone number, which I called. A woman answered. Luckily, it was Mrs. Jacobs.

"You're his wife?" I asked.

"Yes sir, I am," she said.

I was thrilled. "Mrs. Jacobs, I am so glad I found you," I told her. "Can you please sign these closing documents on behalf of your husband—they allow for the wife to sign. I would appreciate it so much. I'll even drive out there [to Palm Springs]."

"Oh, you said this is to help Jeff out?" she asked nicely.

"Yes!" I said.

"Well. You know I would love to do that for you …"

I cut her short, "Great!"

Then she cut *me* off. "*But* I've been separated from that
snake-eyed sonofabitch for 11 years," she told me, "and
I'll burn in hell before I sign anything to help him out."
The minute I heard that, I dropped everything and jumped
the jet for Palm Springs.

That's the important fourth step to the narrative pattern building the intrigue frame: *Get the man to the edge of the jungle, but
don't get him out of it.* In other words, the intrigue is created by
the fact that there's no final resolution.

To hold intrigue and make it work as an emotional event, a hot
cognition, I don't complete the story (although it has a truly great
ending, and it will always come up later) and instead move to the
next frame in the stack: the prize frame.

Hot Cognition 2: The Prize Frame

As I mentioned in Chapter 2, the prize frame—or *prizing*—let's you
position yourself as the most important party in the deal, not the
people on the other side of the table. Successful prizing *flips the
frame.* Even though you are pitching the deal—it results in the target chasing you, trying to win *your* attention.

A simple example of the prize frame comes from my trip to the
Helen Woodward Animal Shelter in Rancho Santa Fe, California—
one of the first times I recognized my own power disrupted and
status seized and watched as the frame *flipped on me.* On entering
the animal shelter, I had the classic hero's frame, announcing, "I'm
here to rescue a homeless, abandoned dog." It was true. The dog
that impressed me the most would win the prize—moving in with
me and getting free food and medical care for life. Soon I found
the dog I liked and was ready to pay the fee and complete the
rescue. Spot seemed like a good name. But wait!

"Excuse me, sir."

It was the "Adoption Counselor." She was in her early 20s, and if she was your sister, you'd tell her to use less hair gel and lose the purple glitter eye shadow.

"What kind of home do you run?" she asked. "Do you have young children? What kind of job do you have? If you're back-yard isn't big enough, we don't recommend a pet like this. And who will take care of the animal when you are at work? What's their number, and what's your income level?"

This was wild. A 23-year-old volunteer with pink streaks in her hair was telling me I might not be a suitable rescuer of this home-less mutt. My hero frame was smashed. Now I was busy defend-ing myself. Giving examples of how I really was a good person.

I answered her questions. Once she gave the nod, I was ready to pay the fee and rescue the animal. Wait! Next, I had to fill out an application. Then I was told to come back in a few hours to see whether I was approved. I came in the hero, and the shelter turned me into a supplicant. Now I was begging to be considered a good enough citizen to rescue a homeless, abandoned animal, of unknown potty skills. I became the commodity, and Spot became the prize. The shelter had flipped the frame.

Let's continue with an example of using the prize frame in a pitch. Because it's specific to my business, pitching deals, I'll start with a detailed example and follow up with a more generic pattern that you can use to develop your own prize frame. What follows can be used toward the end of the pitch session:

"Guys, I'm glad I was able to find some free time to come here and show you my deal. I don't always get to meet the buyers. I know we're having fun here, but I have to wrap up. I have another meeting. We are busy, and there just aren't many deals like this— and obviously none that include me—and I'm fortunate to be in demand. Getting serious for a moment, I do have to choose which investors to let in and which to turn away. Before things go any further here, I need to figure out who you people really are. Yeah, we have your bios and know your reputation. But we have to be cautious about who we bring on board. And I have to sell you to my partner, Joshua—who is going to want to know why I think you would be good partners. *Can you give me that—can you tell me why we would enjoy working with you?*"

So what have I done in such a statement? I've delivered the prize frame, and the basic elements include

1. I have one of the better deals in the market.
2. I am choosy about who I work with.
3. It seems like I could work with you, but really, I need to know more.
4. Please start giving me some materials on yourself.
5. I still need to figure out if we would work well together and be good partners.
6. What did your last business partners say about you?
7. When things go sideways in a deal, how do you handle it?
8. My existing partners are choosy.

The prize frame is a hot cognition that signals the target's croc brain that you are strong, you are not needy, and you are not going to supplicate for a deal.

Dr. Robert Zajonc, writing in *The American Psychologist*, describes the importance of these hot cognitions and the importance of these emotional processes. He suggests, for example, that it's not really important for us to know if someone has just said, "You are a friend" or "You are a fiend." What you really need to know is whether the statement was made with *affection* or *contempt*. Whether the word was *friend* or *fiend* is the cold part of the message. It doesn't matter. Affection or contempt is the hot part.

Researchers found that 22 times as much information is given in the hot part of the message.

Unlike some of the other frames, the prize frame relies a great deal on how strong your conviction is. In the pattern noted earlier, I've given you the external formula for the prize frame—which is what you say to the target. However, the prize frame doesn't come only from words that you say. It's how you're organized internally. Here's the internal pattern, the words you say to yourself to fully activate and deploy the prize frame:

> I am the prize.
> You are trying to impress me.
> You are trying to win my approval.

Over time, as you get good at this stuff, you'll begin to see that the prize frame does not rely on words and explanations. It's more about the strength of your convictions about who or what is the prize.

Hot Cognition 3: The Time Frame

When I was selling a deal called *Geomark* to Boeing, I used this version of the time frame:

"Guys, my company, Geomark, is a great deal, and you can't bluff me about what you are thinking; I know you agree. Consider the situation we're in. We are here for a third meeting at your corporate headquarters. Right now I'm looking at your team: four Boeing executives, three engineers, and two of your consultants. Why are you here in force? Because you love the deal. And you should love it. The deal is hot, that's no secret, and I've never used this fact to pressure you, but we can't ignore it either. For this reason, we have all got to make a decision about the deal in the next week. Why one week? This time constraint is not under my control; it's the market working. It's harsh but true: We have to decide by July 18 if you're in or out."

The effect of time on decision making has been researched for 100 years, and nothing has changed about human nature in that time: In nearly all instances, *the addition of time pressure to a decision-making event reduces decision quality.* It is true, for instance, that you can get someone to buy a car more easily if you tell him that the sale ends at the end of the day. Why does this strategy work so well? *There's a scarcity bias in the brain, and potential loss of a deal triggers fear.* But just because imposing scarcity works well isn't a recommendation to use it—we don't want to taint our deal with the whiff of cheap 1980's sales tactics. We want the target to see us as a professional agent. To trust us. So I tend not to use much time pressure at all. Extreme time pressure feels forced and cutrate. But the truth is that time is a factor in every deal. You have to find the right balance between fairness and pressure and set a real time constraint.

Here's the time frame pattern you can use and follow:

"Guys, nobody likes time pressure. I don't like it, and you don't like it. No one does. But good deals with strong fundamentals are like an Amtrak train, or more like a *deal train.* They stop at the station, pick up investors, and have a set departure time. And when it's time—the train has to leave the station.

"You have plenty of time to decide if you like me—and if you want this deal. If you don't love it, there's no way you should do it; we all know that.

"But this deal is bigger than me, or you or any one person; the deal is going ahead. There's a critical path, a real timeline that everyone has to work with. So we need to decide by the 15th."

That's it. You don't have to do any more. With just that simple pattern, the time constraint is set. You don't have to be overt or aggressive with time pressure. Every single person knows what you're talking about when you say the train is leaving the station at such and such date and time.

Hot Cognition 4: The Moral Authority Frame

Robert Zajonc, the thought leader on hot cognitions, once wrote, "We evaluate each other constantly, we evaluate each others' behaviors and we evaluate the motives and consequences of that behavior." And this, of course, is the key to the reason we stack frames. Because we are going to be evaluated no matter what happens and what we do, let's get the evaluation we want, something Zajonc calls *wanting*.

So, while it's tempting to get caught up in the best way to explain the financial mumbo-jumbo and how to best demo our products, the heart of the matter is that you have to do what it takes to create this wanting. There may be other factors that contribute to our effectiveness in the pitch, but certainly one of the most important is getting this wanting to happen. How is it done? To create a desire in the target's mind and to go on from the pitch to the hookpoint, every presenter has to use hot cognitions to create wanting and desire.

Until a wanting evaluation is in the target's croc brain, the information you are giving is largely being ignored or at least not making a big impression.

Now that we've gone through prize frames, intrigue frames, and time frames and their uses, here is another example that will deepen your understanding of how to use frames to create hot cognitions and wanting.

The Morality Frame in Practice   The most powerful politicians in the world have people underneath them who will do exactly what they are told. Each has phalanx of subordinates who do his or her bidding.

Take the president of the United States. If he orders a precision air strike on a clandestine enemy stronghold, a succession of people underneath him will execute his order, all the way down to the pilot in the F-22. The president can lead us into a war or, with a few pen strokes, sign a bill that will affect millions. His frame, in most of his encounters, is stronger than that of nearly any opposition.

The president, like many other world leaders, isn't used to being told what to do. Think about what one has to go through just to become president, how many personal attacks you suffer, and the constant political reframing of things you have said. Once president, though, you may have one of the most sophisticated and strongest frames in modern history. Yet there is one person whose direction the president will follow, almost blindly. When David Scheiner says to Barack Obama, turn around and take your clothes off—he does it without question.

In every social situation, there are basic, human, hardwired functions. Let's call them *ritual elements* of social interaction. Every person navigates the world through social encounters. In each further contact with other people, as we have been discussing, each person brings a frame, which is a viewpoint or perspective. It doesn't matter if the person intends to bring a frame, he always will find that he has done so. All social encounters are framed. In light of this, when we think about it, not only do physicians such as Dr. David Scheiner tell us what to do, their frame is so powerful that we are nearly helpless in its presence.

In fact, the doctor frame may be the most powerful frame in the world. *Really?* The most powerful frame in the world? Let's explore.

If we want to stay alive, we all follow our doctor's orders. And we have deep respect for the medical profession. Physicians, cardiologists, radiologists, internists, and surgeons—these are people who can save our life or the life of a loved one. So we have an embedded script that we follow when we deal with medical professionals. When the surgeon stands, we sit. If the surgeon waves his hand toward the table, we go sit on it, uncomfortably trying to cover up private areas.

Literally, when the surgeon does anything, we are programmed to react. We react to the surgeon automatically. He doesn't react to us. We obey him. The surgeon only nods appreciatively when we say something but doesn't react.

The consulting surgeon wears whatever he wants, sometimes a nice suit, other times comfortable-looking casual clothes, whereas at the same time we are dressed in a generic green gown, sans underwear, that signifies our low situational status. If we were seen anywhere in public in this ridiculous gown, it would cause us emotional scarring. The surgeon is wealthy, and has all the accoutrements of status: a prestigious degree, a respected position, and an expertise that took nearly 20 years to acquire, and he literally has the power to determine life or death.

We are hardwired to follow this script. Most of us, but not all of us. Certainly not Mother Teresa.

In December 1991, Mother Teresa entered Scripps Clinic and Research Foundation in La Jolla, California, where she was treated for bacterial pneumonia and heart problems. With such a notable world figure under their care, doctors and surgeons rushed in to meet her. And frames collided.

The doctor's frame has three rules:

Rule 1: Do what I say.
Rule 2: Defer to my expertise.
Rule 3: Accept my conclusions about life (and death).

However, when encountering Mother Teresa, the doctors found a person who did not follow the script or fall into the frame.

Here was Mother Teresa's frame:

1. Material wealth is worth nothing.
2. Life and death isn't critical.
3. Help the downtrodden.
4. A rich man is less likely to enter the kingdom of heaven than a camel is to pass through the eye of a needle.

Her frame is not powered by wealth or expertise—instead, by a high moral authority: Help the downtrodden! Life and death isn't critical!

As doctor after doctor met with Mother Teresa, their strong frames collapsed like a series of dominoes. She did not react to their status or their control over life and death. After all, even death was not one of her primary concerns, and she had often ignored doctors' orders in the past. And as they fell into her frame, something remarkable happened: These doctors could not impress her. Their power frame was disrupted.

This is why she so easily convinced American doctors to do something that they hadn't previously considered. Before coming to La Jolla—an affluent seaside community in north San Diego, Mother Teresa had visited Tijuana, a city across the U.S.-Mexican border where poverty is severe. It was there she learned of the huge disparity between the United States and Mexico, between Tijuana and La Jolla, between the haves and the have-nots. So, as these doctors fell over themselves to visit her, she sensed a tremendous opportunity. She asked the doctors what they were doing to give back. And then she asked them if they had ever seen the medical facilities, a mere 25 miles away, in Tijuana. Most of them said no.

She then asked each doctor to add his or her name to a sign-up sheet outside her room, pledging to donate time and resources to help mobile medical clinics in Tijuana.

The doctors, who were used to having the dominant frame, couldn't impress Mother Teresa with any of the usual trappings of success. They could only do it by pledging their time and expertise to her cause.

When it was time for her to leave the hospital, after 20 days at Scripps, Mother Teresa had imposed her frame on the richest, smartest, best-educated, and highest social class in southern California, and this was evidenced by the sheer number of doctors who had pledged their time to help out in Tijuana. And the doctors? Without any noticeable effort, their frames had been shaken, broken, and disrupted. With the high-status surgeon power frame disrupted, Mother Teresa's frame took over. According to the *Los Angeles Times*, "On January 16, 1992, Mother Teresa of Calcutta was released from the Scripps Clinic and Research Foundation hospital, after securing a pledge from doctors and nurses to set up a volunteer network of mobile medical clinics to serve the poor of Tijuana."

When asked whether she was going to take better care of herself, she replied, "Oh, sure."

Reality Is Waiting to Be Framed

A hot cognition—or a series of hot cognitions—is a fast method for getting the target's croc brain to want you and your big idea.

But this is not a 'sales technique. Stacking frames is not going to work, in my opinion, if you view it as just another type of sales tactic. Those old-fashioned sales techniques are about chasing the neocortex with features and benefits and rational explanations. "Selling" tempts you to do the three things I dislike the most: (1) supplicate; (2) make rational appeals to the neocortex, and (3) ask invasive questions. Hot cognitions, on the other hand, do not hit the target like a sales technique.

- *Hot cognitions are primal.* Whenever there's a rush of excitement, it's hard to get the neocortex to do any work at all. To protect us from potential physical or social threat, the croc brain hijacks brain function. No analysis gets done. As a result, it's much easier and natural to react to what's hot and vivid and moving right in front of us.
- *Hot cognitions are unavoidable.* You might be able to control the *expression* of emotion, but there's no way you can get out of the path of having and experiencing it.
- *Hot cognitions tend to be instant and enduring.* Do you like the movie you just watched? Do you like the new model of Ford Mustang? Do you like eating snails? You never sat down to analyze these things; they're obviously hot cognitions—you got a sense of these things the moment you encountered them.

Hot versus Cold Cognition

Maybe the best way to define hot versus cold cognition is to compare it to chocolate and spinach. You know the cold, hard facts. Spinach is good for you, it has lots of nutrients, and you should be eating more of it. But when offered a piece of chocolate instead, you go for it.

The acid test of whether your pitch goes well will be: Does the target want to buy your stuff, be a part of your team, or invest in your idea?

How much thinking about your presentation does your target need before he or she forms a preference about it? How "fully and completely" must an idea be presented and thought about, and how much rational analysis needs to be completed before the target decides: "good" or "bad"? I argue here that as you approach the end of your pitch, you don't need to wait for an evaluation, or the target will wander off into a cold cognition process and think about you: did we like him, did we like his deal? Instead, stack the four frames, trigger hot cognitions, and create the instant evaluation that ought to be *wanting*.

If hot cognitions targeted at the croc brain are so powerful, why do most people make presentations in the cold cognition style targeted to the neocortex? Here's why I think people go this way: Our faculties of reason tell us that the neocortex is way smarter than the croc brain. We think that if we create a message in our own smart neocortex, it should be sent to the target's neocortex, which will do a better job of understanding the pitch. It makes sense to think this way because the neocortex really *is* an insanely capable problem solver. It has awesome language and math and creative abilities. It's a Swiss Army knife of mental ability.

By contrast, if the neocortex is like a Swiss Army knife, then the croc brain is a like a rubber mallet—best for simple jobs only. It works on only a few emotions, and those are very limited in scope and range. The croc brain almost seems too simple to "get" our smart ideas. We think, *Who are we going to trust this decision to, the target's infinitely capable neocortex or the emotional and simplistic croc brain?* Our intuition tells us to trust the neocortex. But that's not the right choice. Let's return to the essential idea from Chapter 1: *No pitch or message is going to get to the logic center of the other person's brain without passing through the survival filters of the crocodile brain system first. And because of the way we evolved, those filters make pitching anything extremely difficult.*

By this point, you know what I'm going to say next: Focus your energy on getting the target's croc brain to want your product. Because, at best, no matter how much you try to sell to the neocortex—*it can only "like" your idea.*

A *hot cognition* is the inner certainty of "knowing" something that comes through feeling it. A *cold cognition* is the certainty of "knowing" something is good or bad by having evaluated it.

As we've said before, *hot cognitions are extremely fast.* Hot cognitions develop through the ancient brain structures—the brain stem and the midbrain—our croc brain. Cold cognitions are analytical and develop in the neocortex. Cold cognitions are calculated and take time to suggest a solution—this is how the neocortex goes about its business—it aggregates information over time and solves problems. You've heard the expression, "Just give me the cold, hard facts?" This is what is meant by a cold cognition, the labor-intensive processing of facts through a decision matrix.

You can trigger a hot cognition instantly, but cold cognition can take hours or days. Most presentations are set up to take the target down the path of a cold cognition. They try to justify the big idea with facts and information.

Hot cognitions encode value. It's the anticipation of a large financial gain that is emotionally compelling to the target. Actually receiving it is not nearly as exciting. As one researcher noted, "The human brain acquired its reward-reinforcement system for food, drink, ornaments, and other items of cultural value long before money was discovered." The brain thinks of money as it does of food, ornaments, and drugs and records the utility that can be collected by using it only indirectly. There's no cash register or balance sheet up there.

George Soros once wrote: "The philosophers of the Enlightenment put their faith in reason; ... and they expected reason to provide a full and accurate picture of reality. Reason was supposed to work like a searchlight, illuminating a reality that lay there, passively awaiting discovery."

As we have been discussing, reality isn't waiting to be discovered—it's waiting to be framed. By stacking four frames quickly one after the other, you can achieve the hot cognition in the target—helping the target to discover a *wanting*. Yet, once the frame stacking is complete, we've got the target's attention for about another 30 seconds. And it still can all go wrong. We have to find, in that brief time, a way to translate the target's desire into action. But how? What do you do now?

Chapter 6

Eradicating Neediness

Over the years, I have faced a lot of rejection. And the disturbing thing about rejection is that you never really get used to it. It's natural and even unavoidable to feel disappointment when you get a "No." We all do. What's certain is that none of us like being rejected. We want to avoid it. In high-stakes situations, we're nearly always anxious about it.

As businesspeople, friends, neighbors and citizens, we believe that when we need something from another person, there is a thin line of empathy that runs through all human hearts. We believe that we'll be treated well by others *just because*. But there isn't, and we won't. So we nearly always become anxious and needy.

Showing signs of neediness is about the worst thing you can do to your pitch. It's incredibly bad for frame control. It erodes status. It freezes your hot cognitions. It topples your frame stacks.

If you talk to investment bankers, the pros that make million dollar decisions almost daily, they'll tell you—validation-seeking behavior (neediness) is the number one deal killer.

Four Pitches, No Room for Mistakes

Twelve years ago, I was trying to raise money for a technology company that I had also invested in. The company was quickly burning through cash. I needed to find a big-time investor, so each day I'd make up to 50 calls to leading venture-capital (VC) firms. I talked to a lot of receptionists and secretaries, and I got a lot of voice-mail action. But nobody was excited enough to return my call.

My company had a great idea, but it was difficult to explain over the phone. I needed face time to explain it, so I was desperate to simply land a meeting. I continued to be persistent, and the following week, I got a few people to pick up and tried to pitch them by phone. That didn't go well. Bill Reichert at Garage Technology Ventures told me, "I have no idea why anyone would want to build it, use it, or invest in it." Ron Fisher, at Softbank VC said, "Do yourself a favor, son. Try a different idea."

I reached Vinod Khosla at VC firm Kleiner Perkins, and he quickly transferred me to his analyst; an obvious dead end. I was getting nothing but rejections from the largest VC firms in North America. I questioned whether I should continue. It was a constant battle in my mind, press on or give up? But I'd passed the point of no return.

It sounds simple, but no greater truth exists in business today: Persistence pays. So I persisted. Eventually, I was able to get four big pitches lined up with top-tier VC firms. But setting a meeting is just step one of a two-step process. You have to impress and persuade, or you go home with nothing, which I was getting good at—the *going home with nothing part*, that is.

This was a confidence killer—I knew I was good at pitching, but for some reason, my pitches were failing. And now, I was in big trouble. I'm embarrassed to say it, but it's a matter of public record (UCLA's Anderson School of Management uses a case study on this deal in its MBA program), I had less than $1,000 in my account, and my company was down to one final pitch, one last chance with a major VC firm, before the cash ran out and our doors closed for good.

I tried to develop a theory to explain what was going wrong—but I came up with nothing. I had a lot of self-doubt. *What was I doing wrong? There must be something.* Rather than make the same mistakes again in my final pitch, I decided to regroup and reorganize myself. A bit humbled, I went back to my former employer to speak with the senior partner, Peter.

Peter was another master of the universe type, and I had helped him put together a number of big deals that had made him a lot of money. If anyone would help me, it would be Peter.

I shut his office door and sat down, unsure if he was going to help or just lecture me. After I thanked him for seeing me, he said, "Oren, I've watched your career very carefully, and while I see flashes of brilliance, you know I've also identified plenty of problems over the years."

"Right," I said, bracing for the lecture that was to come.

"You're just inconsistent," he went on. "Sometimes you're fantastic. Other times you let us down. We were always unsure which Oren we were going to get on what day."

I really wanted to defend myself, but I knew that nodding my head and staying quiet was the best approach—for now.

"Let's go back," he continued. "Two years ago, you seemed invincible. You had just helped us close Somatex, the most profitable deal in our history."

How could I forget? Without me, that deal would have died. Guys got rich on that deal, thanks to me. "I remember it," I said.

"You were a few deals away from becoming a partner."

Becoming a partner, the most coveted position at any investment bank, had indeed been within my grasp. I'd also landed a sweet deal with Hershey's that made the firm over $1 million. And my work helped the firm to close several other big deals. The competition could only watch in awe and envy as we put together a great run.

"You were strong and confident and acing deals that we really liked," Peter said, "But. ..." His voice trailed off.

I'm sure he was still disappointed and hurt that I had abruptly left the firm, seduced by the promise of the Internet.

"I'm sorry," I told him. "But I'm here because I'm in dire straits. I have one more chance, or this whole thing is going to implode."

He looked at me and nodded.

For the next hour, I replayed the three failed VC meetings while Peter asked me questions. Eventually, his eyebrows lifted, he smiled, and he broke into a laugh. He stopped me midsentence.

"I know why you seem to have lost your edge," he said.

"Why?" I asked.

He allowed the moment to build and finally said, "Because you're out there, on your own, and you know there's no safety net. Son, you're going to these meetings ... *needy*."

I snapped to attention. Of course. Classic validation-seeking behavior. Signals of desperation. No investor wants to work with a needy company run by an entrepreneur who is almost out of cash! Sure, the investor knows you need money, but giving a hint of neediness or any sign of desperation, plainly put, is like saying, "I'm holding a bomb that could go off at any minute." Everyone will respond by going on the defensive. Their first reaction is—Run!

Self-protection is an unconscious reaction that comes from the crocodile brain. This is the critical lesson of my failed pitches and the key to understanding why otherwise good deals can fail to impress the target. Neediness triggers fear and uncertainty, causing the target's croc brain to take over—but not in a good way. Its goal is to prevent further threat by effectively blocking out the higher-level brain, which likes to debate and consider and analyze. No time for that. Threats require immediate action.

Neediness is a signal of threat. If you display neediness, it is perceived as just the kind of threat that the crocodile brain wants to avoid. Neediness results in avoidance.

I knew that Peter was right, and I listened carefully as he gave me advice on eliminating neediness. And although my situation was desperate, he told me to "Get some game." In other words, find some source of inner strength, confidence, and poise. Easy to say. Hard to do.

When pitches work well, we tend to believe that it was our great idea that impressed the target. Or that our sublime explanation of the big idea was impressive and convincing. However, when pitches fail, we see it through a different lens. In such cases, we believe that the problem lies with the target, not us. We believe that the target somehow couldn't see the value of the big idea or that he was the wrong target. But pitches can fail for reasons that are hidden from view.

I thought back to my previous pitch, the third of the three failures. A VC group in Silicon Valley was interested in my deal. During my call, the representative said, "Your executive summary was good, we like your idea, and under the right leadership, this could become a large company and eventually go public. We'd like you to come up Tuesday to pitch the partnership."

I made plans to fly north and thought that this was my big break. When we got there, though, the circumstances felt familiar. I'd been in this position before. It was just another one-hour meeting in an anonymous office building overlooking a freeway. The conference room looked virtually the same as every other one I had pitched in: black leather chairs, a long conference table, a white-board, and an easel.

Thinking back on those days, if there's anything that reminds me of deal making, it's the acrid whiff of dry-erase markers. In 1999, no deal could be pitched properly without extensive—and highly abstract—whiteboard diagrams.

Now, when I was pitching, I spoke clearly and made my points elegantly. I maintained eye contact with the targets, exuding calm confidence. My voice rose and fell with dramatic timbre as I drew a chart on their whiteboard so artistic that, had it been preserved, it would today be hanging in the modern art hall of the Getty Museum.

Before I knew it, 30 minutes had gone by. Although I felt that there was much more to say, the targets were glancing at their watches. I knew it was time to wrap up, and with nearly perfect comedic timing, I delivered a joke, and laughter filled the room. I'd nailed the pitch.

Now I found myself in that awkward two-minute period that every presenter must face after finishing his or her pitch. This is a dangerous *beta trap* and the easiest time to screw things up. Here is where small mistakes are amplified into deal killers. Slight mis-steps can erase all the good work you've done in the last 20 min-utes. And it's unnerving because there's always an unspoken directive: You need something from the target. Money.

So, during the end of that third pitch, in front of some of the best venture capitalists in Silicon Valley, I became anxious and needy while I explained:We need a lot of your money, and we need it fast. At that point, I realized how high the stakes were. If these people said no, it would be my third rejection in a row. And the company would have almost no options left. I felt scared and anxious. I said things like:

- "Do you still think it's a good deal?"
- "So, what do think?"
- "We can sign a deal right away if you want us to."

This is the purest form of validation seeking and the most lethal form of neediness. And that was the end of that opportunity. Just that fast, the target's excitement turned to fear and anxiety. And of course, I failed to get a term sheet or an investment offer.

Why It's Important to Eradicate Neediness

Plain and simple, neediness equals weakness. Broadcasting weakness by seeking validation is often a death sentence. This may sound harsh, but it is true. Neediness—displaying so-called validation-seeking behaviors—will affect all social interactions dramatically.

It is almost redundant to criticize the concept of validation seeking any further. Simply put, there's almost no way to get through the postpitch time period if you are needy. Let's define validation seeking and neediness and talk about how to get through the two-minute beta trap or any other point where you might be showing neediness.

What Causes Neediness?

You can tell when you are losing your audience because their growing discomfort is easy to read. They glance at their watches, turn their bodies away from you, cough nervously, and/or close the folder they had been leafing through. There are lots of outward signs.

When you notice that audience members are uncomfortable, you feel yourself losing the deal. Your anxiety and insecurity start turning into fear, and you begin falling into acceptance-seeking behaviors.

The experience of feeling disappointment creates problems that need to be considered carefully. When we feel even a touch of disappointment, our first reflexive reaction is to cure it by seeking validation, which, of course, broadcasts neediness to the audience.

Now our brain is subconsciously thinking, "If I can just get them to agree to do the deal with me, everything will be okay." This is what our brain wants to relieve the stress and fear caused by rejection. If we are lucky and the target decides to give us the deal, all is well again. We instantly feel better, our anxiety fades, our heart-rate returns to normal, and we feel in control.

However, in the panic moment caused by that flash of disappointment, we couldn't help but signal neediness to our target. Chances are good that he noticed it and will not respond by giving us what we want. What happens then? Further rejection poses the threat for an emotional catastrophe.

In practice, here is how we fall into validation-seeking behaviors:

1. When we want something that only the target can give us (money, an order, a job,) we set the stage for neediness.
2. When we need cooperation from the target and can't get it, it's frustrating and causes us anxiety. And audiences, at some point, always become uncooperative. Audience members turn their attention elsewhere—usually by texting, scanning e-mail, or taking phone calls. They allow interruptions by people coming in and out of the meeting room. Or they cut us short—before we've made our key points.
3. Neediness is created inside of us when we firmly believe that the target can make us feel good by accepting our

pitch and by saying "Yes." When we set ourselves up to need the target to accept us, we have trapped ourselves. The more we want the target's desired behavior to occur, the more neediness we broadcast, and the less likely the target is to give us what we want. It's a downward spiral.

4. Finally, validation-seeking behaviors are triggered in us when the target seems uninterested in our pitch, begins to withdraw, or shifts his or her attention to something else. At that moment, we have a natural fear response, and the potential for an involuntary expression of neediness is high. Fear and anxiety are emotions that are both natural and reflexive, and they are very difficult to manage. Even the most common social rituals are loaded with situations that can trip us up, so you really need to pay attention to avoid outward signs of neediness—a reaction that surrenders your status and frame dominance.

Counteract Your Validation-Seeking Behaviors

One dramatic way to eradicate neediness involves going into every social interaction with a strong time frame that you are prepared to use at any moment. This frame communicates, loudly and clearly, that you are needed somewhere else.

But this is just a part of a broader, more comprehensive solution to eradicating neediness. Here's the basic formula:

1. Want nothing.
2. Focus only on things you do well.
3. Announce your intention to leave the social encounter.

Executing these three steps will calm down the fear circuitry in your own brain. Your increased heart rate, perspiration, rapid breathing, and anxiety will subside slowly. Once under control, you'll impress others and make them actually come after you. Most important, the willingness to withdraw demonstrates a self-control, strength, and confidence that most targets will greatly admire.

To better appreciate the importance of controlling validation-seeking behaviors, let's take a closer look at the way others have solved this problem.

In the film *The Tao of Steve*, the lead character, Dex, also employs the withdrawal technique to maintain a high status in social situations. This technique is part of a larger Taoist philosophy that Dex uses to guide his life.

Dex is an elementary school teacher's assistant who lives in Santa Fe, New Mexico, with several roommates. He has a huge belly, he smokes pot, and his wild, unkempt look is the opposite of Madison Avenue's image of the American male. Looking at Dex from the outside, you'd assume that he is *not* a social success. But surprisingly, the opposite is true.

Dex is a practitioner of the Taoist philosophy, but with an ingenious twist (which I'll explain in a moment). Taoism is an Eastern philosophical and religious tradition that originated in China around 500 B.C. It is based on the writings of the philosopher Lao-Tsu. As in Buddhism, there is a heavy emphasis on connecting with the universe and controlling your desires.

In the movie, Dex has developed his own derivative version of the Tao that draws its inspiration from popular culture. He calls it the "Tao of Steve"—named for three guys named Steve who embody all the coolness and social poise that Dex is seeking. The three Steves are Steve McQueen, Steve Austin, and Steve McGarrett.

McQueen, the so-called King of Cool, rode an antihero persona to become the highest-paid actor of his generation. His roles in movies such as the *Magnificent Seven, The Great Escape,* and *Bullitt* won him a legion of female admirers and also cemented his reputation as a "man's man."

Steve McGarrett (Jack Lord) was the detective in charge of the elite crime unit on the popular 1960s show *Hawaii Five-O*. He was a no-nonsense, dedicated investigator who always stayed one step ahead of the bad guys.

Steve Austin (Lee Majors) was the bionic man in the 1970s hit, *The Six Million Dollar Man*. Austin was a former astronaut who survived an experimental plane crash. He was rebuilt with bionic parts and became an operative for a covert government agency.

All three were noted for being cool without really trying. The actors helped convey this feeling by maintaining poise in pressure situations. They never got flustered, even with the bad guys closing in.

Dex believed that the three Steves attracted admirers not because they had cool cars or bionic legs, but rather because they understood the three main rules of the Tao:

> *Eliminate your desires.* It's not necessary to want things. Sometimes you have to let them come to you.
> *Be excellent in the presence of others.* Show people one thing that you are very good at.
> *Withdraw.* At a crucial moment, when people are expecting you to come after them, pull away.

The Tao of Steve is the perfect philosophy to use when you finish your pitch. Use it to stifle the urge to seek approval from your audience. People want what they can't have. So, when you finish your pitch, deny your audience. Start to pull away. In so doing, you banish insecurity and trigger a powerful prizing effect on your audience. They will come to you.

The Final Pitch

Now, finally, it was the day of my fourth and final pitch. Six months ago, I had hundreds of thousands in my bank account. Now I had $468, enough for half of a payment on my Porsche, and that was if I didn't pay rent or eat. Nevertheless, in my head, I ran a constant audio loop: *I don't need these people; they need me. I am the prize.*

I stood in front of Enterprise Partners, the largest VC firm south of Silicon Valley. It was nearly 4 p.m., and the people inside were ready to go home. I needed to electrify them, light up the room, and most important, I needed to forget that this was *do or die.* If they sensed any desperation, my partner and I would go home busted. This was my last chance.

I walked into a room of tired-looking investors. They'd been hearing pitches all day; none of them even bothered to say hello. It was unnerving.

They asked me a series of hostile questions. They wondered aloud if the market was big enough or if there was too much competition already. One of them actually laughed at our idea. And to make matters worse, the partner who brought us through the door (*sponsored us,* so to speak) questioned whether we should even be an Internet company, instead, suggesting that we settle on making PC software, which was the equivalent of saying, I no longer support this deal.

But none of that mattered. I delivered the knock-down, drag-out, bare-knuckled superpitch. Exactly 20 minutes of hardcore finance in a sexy Internet wrapper. At the end, I continued with my plan to run the prize frame and qualify them.

I made three points. Here's what I told the Enterprise investors:

1. This deal will be fully subscribed in the next 14 days.

2. We don't need VC money, but we want a big name on our cap sheet that will strengthen our initial public offering (IPO) registration.
3. I think you guys are interesting, but are you really the right investor? We need to know more about you and the relationships and brand value your firm can bring to our deal.

That was it. I was totally spent. At that moment, I couldn't muster enough mental power or energy to do anything but sit still and be silent. Now it was my turn to be the stone-faced gnome. I just sat there, with no trace of validation-seeking behavior, no neediness, waiting for them to react to me.

To my surprise, they fully engaged with me and in minutes had committed to the deal. They wanted what I had. I'd redeemed myself with a great opening and finished the pitch with confidence and poise, and the whole thing came together perfectly.

We sat in the room for another hour and discussed all the variables. We came up with a huge $14 million valuation—$6 million more than I had expected.

Yes, my bank account had dwindled to $468, but the next day, Enterprise Partners officially agreed to invest. And a few days later, they wired $2.1 million into my account. I remember going to the ATM and getting a balance slip so that I could see the $2.1 million printed on it. Thirty days later, Enterprise completed the financing with an additional $4 million.

Despite the difficulties and hard work, going after a deal is a thrill. Sure, I do it because I want the results—the loan, the job, the money, the deal ... whatever. But that's not the only reason. I chase these things because the adventure excites me. All deal makers know: There's a king-of-the-world moment when we close a deal that is never forgotten. It's the satisfaction of preparing for a high-stakes meeting, giving a mouth-watering pitch, and with a chest full of confidence, getting the deal.

Over time, I would have had many fewer of these moments if I had not learned: *Never be needy!*

Chapter 7

Case Study: The Airport Deal

This is the story of a pitch so massive and so high stakes that in order to tell it properly, I'll need to tell you what happened in the months leading up to the day of the pitch. There is perhaps no other single deal I've ever been involved with that better demonstrates the ideas at the core of my method and why it works. If you find that the story borders on the cinematic at times, well, that's what it was like to be there, and that's what it's like when you're playing with hundreds of millions and there's so much at stake. Let's begin.

I was 100 miles away from Los Angeles and in no hurry to return to the city. I had a very good reason, too: Business was dead. The collapse of the U.S. economy had seized the credit markets, freezing deals for more than a year. After pitching nearly nonstop for more than five years, I found myself with nothing to pitch—literally nothing. This lack of action was frustrating because at heart, I like the adrenaline rush that comes from playing this game. That's why I do it.

I get the same adrenaline rush from action sports as I do in a board-room—where I've raised more than $400 million.

Then it all went away—*Poof!*—as the economy soured and the deal window shut. It was clear, after a full year, that it wasn't going to return to normal—for a long time. That's why I'd decided to get away—from all of it. The deal business had been very good to me, and I was in a position to do anything I wanted. I told friends, colleagues, everyone that I was done. *"I'm hanging up my guns,"* I said.

And now I was due for some serious downtime in the middle of nowhere to figure out what I'd be doing next in life. A one-week vacation to the Anza-Borrego Desert had turned into two, and I was enjoying all that the tiny town of Ocotillio Wells had to offer—which wasn't much. It was a Monday in December, a dry 78 degrees, and most of the weekend guests had now retreated from this outpost in southern California on the east end of the Salton Sea. The solitude felt good. Most of my day was spent mountain biking and relaxing on a mesa. I snapped pictures of the sun as it settled behind a bluff. Life was good. And I was oblivious to the fact that someone was desperately trying to reach me.

A Monster Deal

Across the mountain range that separates the high desert from the coast, in Los Angeles, Sam Greenberg was that someone. He sat in his office, frustrated, wondering what it would take to get in touch with me. I had pretty much made myself unreachable—my phone had been switched off, my e-mail autoresponder was switched on, and almost no one knew where I was staying.

Greenberg had a deal on the table, a big deal—10 figures, $1 billion. He wanted me to be his point man, just like the way things were before the economy collapsed. Greenberg was a man of action. He kept a private jet at Palomar Airport—not as a luxury item but as a tool to get to deals faster than the next guy. He would find me, get the plane in the air, and get me back to work. At least that was his plan, and it served his purpose. An acquaintance finally spilled my hotel information, and Greenberg left a short message on the hotel answering machine.

"I've got a monster deal," he said in a loud voice. "Call me, today. ASAP."

Three hours later, I entered my hotel room and saw the red light flashing—so much for privacy. *Who needs to reach me that badly?* Only a handful of people knew how to get in touch. I listened to Greenberg's message, alternately ignoring it and then wondering about it. *No.* After 10 years of nonstop deal making, I'd sworn off deals. I'd sworn off the industry.

No.

I was resolute, but I owed Greenberg enough to call him back and tell him as much. When he answered the phone, my first word was "No."

"I haven't even told you the deal," Greenberg said.

Greenberg had a natural gift of persuasion and typically got what he wanted, but this time I was sure I wanted no part of it.

"My answer is still no," I said.

"Just listen to me for one minute," Greenberg demanded.

"It's not going to matter," I said. "I've seen about every deal out there—it's a wasteland."

Greenberg told me about a deal right in our backyard. Davis Field, a regional airport on the outskirts of Los Angeles, was being rechristened as a large private fixed-base operator (FBO) as a relief valve for the overflowing Los Angeles air space and would need a whopping $1 billion raised to finance the effort.

"You *can't* turn this one down," Greenberg bellowed. "This is not some shopping center. This is a *friggin' airport!*"

"Sounds great, but I can't do it," I said. "I'm out of the game."

After three or four expletives, Greenberg tried another approach.

"That's fine. I got someone else lined up anyway, so ..." His voice trailed off.

After a long pause, I took the bait. "Who?"

"Barnes."

"Oh, please."

"He can pull it off," Greenberg said. "And on your end, I guess we'll just chalk it up to a missed opportunity. You're gonna kick yourself."

Greenberg indeed had another guy lined up, but everyone knew that Paul Barnes was not exactly "the best."

Greenberg decided to stop his pursuit—for now.

"Have fun sticking your head in the sand while we're doing a monster deal," he added in closing. Then he hung up, not even waiting for a response.

I laughed and thought about the call. Over the years, I'd become hardwired to analyze every pitch to find out what worked and what didn't. Greenberg's pitch meant there was just one deal in a dead market, and that was no reason to unretire. I called the front desk and asked the clerk to hold all calls.

Two weeks went by, and sure enough—Paul Barnes did not perform as expected. Sure, he was confident and had a great analytical mind, but he couldn't think on his feet. If circumstances changed or things got off plan, he spooked easily. When Greenberg suddenly asked him to fly to Chicago on a red-eye for a meeting, Barnes begged off. "I need a few days to prepare," he said.

One of the things my business associates know about me is this: I would go anywhere, anytime to make a deal happen. If a flight was canceled, I'd drive. No cars? I'd take a bus. And after all these years, Greenberg trusted me. He wouldn't think twice about making a strategy change based on my recommendations.

So Greenberg was worried. He had two months to prepare the pitch for the airport selection committee—not just a presentation, but a full-pitch package, complete with a detailed financial analysis and strategy. He knew I could deliver a real face melter of a pitch, a compelling and dramatic story that explained everything. *Why now, why us, critical path, upside, downside, and competitive advantage.* All stuff that I'd done hundreds of times.

After Barnes proved unsuitable for the situation, Greenberg realized that he needed me.

Greenberg Goes to Borrego Springs

Greenberg's Legacy 600 landed at the alarmingly tiny runway in Borrego Springs before 10 a.m., and within 15 minutes, he was in a car, headed to the Borrego Valley Inn. I'd agreed to meet him at noon in the hotel lobby.

It was nearly 10 years earlier that Greenberg had listened to one of my pitches and tried to hire me on the spot. I turned him down, saying I wasn't for hire, but we went on to partner up eventually. Together we made a lot of deals that propelled Greenberg Capital into a premiere position in the financial markets.

Now, the team had disbanded, and no deals were happening.

At 11:54 a.m., he approached the lobby. This was classic Sam Greenberg, who, like the legendary Carthaginian commander

Hannibal, would either find a way or make one. This guy would not fly back without pushing our relationship to the brink. This was just the way he worked.

Shortly after 11:30 a.m., I thought about possible scenarios. Was there anything Sam could say to sway me? Not likely. Was the deal economy coming back any time soon? Also not likely.

There was a certain peace I had now, away from the rat race, not tied down by phones and e-mails. And I didn't miss the grind. Not at all.

It was getting close to noon. I headed to the lobby. Sam was there, dressed casually, sitting on a blue vinyl couch. Both of us were uncomfortable at first—as if meeting for the first time—we both had our game faces on.

"You know I can't let the plane idle on the runway for too long, so pack up and let's head back," Greenberg said with a straight face.

Ahhh, the time frame—it would need to be dealt with.

"At this altitude, after your 25-minute short hop, that jet can idle for three and a half hours in 98 degree heat with a half tank of fuel," I said, cracking Greenberg's power frame in half with the stronger expert frame. "And I'm hungry. It's your turn to buy lunch."

Greenberg countered the expert frame with a prize frame. "You've never made as much money as you have working with me," he calmly replied. "Look at you—you're leaning forward, hanging on every word I say. You're practicality drooling. That's how much you want this deal. It's almost sad."

"Ah, you're throwing a prize frame at me! I taught you too much!" I said, easily handling Greenberg's reframe. "Look, we could do this all afternoon. Forget it. Let's go eat. You're still buying. Follow me."

On the way to the sandwich shop, we continued to frame and reframe and deframe about who would buy a $20 lunch, even though Greenberg's fueled, piloted, and fully staffed jet was on the runway burning $8,400 an hour.

"Let's get back to doing what we always do," Greenberg said, continuing the conversation at the restaurant.

"Market says that's a bad idea," I replied.

This was probably an anticipated objection. He decided to challenge me. Chide me a bit.

"Why exactly did you come here?" he asked. "You just ran away. *You left because you lost your edge*," Greenberg continued.

"There was a point where I thought you might be one of the best," he said. "Now, the only thing next to your name will be ... *quitter*."

That one made me clench my teeth. I stood up and gave him a long stare. I was ready to walk away right there.

"You're mad because I'm right," he said. "Maybe you'll come back with me and prove me wrong. You can't hang out and be a hippie—or whatever you call this—the rest of your life."

I could feel his neediness, and it was clear that I had the upper hand, for the moment. But you never have that upper hand long with Greenberg.

"Give me a minute to think about it," I told him.

The $1 billion figure for this deal was off the charts—I'd been accustomed to pitching deals in the $30 million range. This would be the biggest deal I'd ever put together. And it was only falling into my wheelhouse because the bad economy had sent everyone else scrambling. The fact that Greenberg had flown out to the middle of the desert also gave me a sense of importance—and a notion that loyalty still existed in the cutthroat world of investment banking.

"Let's talk about this," I said finally, looking across at Greenberg. "What exactly are you offering if I get back in the game?"

Greenberg's eyes lit up. The bullying had worked. He now had a hookpoint. It was time to take advantage. For the next 15 minutes, he explained the deal, pitched it actually, and laid out my role in the big picture. Then he closed the deal and sealed it, giving me some reasonable terms and a rare handshake.

Little did I know that Greenberg had withheld a key piece of information—there was a competitor in this pitch—a *big competitor*.

Preparing the Big Pitch

The next day, back in Los Angeles, Greenberg and I got together at Greenberg's high-rise office to discuss an action plan. It was Wednesday. Greenberg came to the meeting knowing that he'd have to mention the competitor. But he waited until the end of the meeting and then sprung it on me.

"Did I mention that Goldhammer is pitching the deal, too?" Greenberg asked.

I almost spit up my coffee.

"What?!"

"Yeah, they have a team on it," Greenberg said. "Relax. It's nobody we can't take down."

"You knew that when you flew out, and you didn't tell me?"

"What does it matter?" Greenberg said, trying to play it down.

"It matters because they beat us most of the time," I said. "Goldhammer is Goldhammer. They have 10 times the resources, and they have the Goldhammer pedigree."

"That's why I got you, so we could beat them," Greenberg said.

"No," I said. "You didn't disclose this, and if you had, I wouldn't have come. I'll go toe to toe with anyone, but this is not a fair fight."

I was seething. Greenberg had purposely withheld this information, and now I felt betrayed. We were up against Goldhammer, who would throw 12 to 15 people at the effort against our 6. But the potential rewards certainly made the effort worth it. If we won the pitch and actually raised the $1 billion for the airport over a period of five years, Greenberg Capital would reap more than $25 million in fees. Of that, I would take 30 percent. So I had a lot to prove, a lot at stake, and a lot to gain. All I had to do was take down Goldhammer and my old arch-rival Timothy Chance.

Meanwhile at Goldhammer

The Goldhammer office in Los Angeles occupies the entire twelfth floor of a gorgeous downtown skyscraper with a view all the way across Hollywood to the Pacific. The floor is decorated throughout with touches from the Orient—a jade dragon, ornate vases, and Japanese flower arrangements. I'd tangled with Goldhammer before, so I'd been in that office. I could picture in my head *exactly* how the company's planning session against my team was going. This is how I envisioned it:

Inside the main conference room, seven people would be gathered to discuss a big deal—a monster deal, the airport deal. The discussion would be led by Bill Miner, a second-generation investment banker who had been hand picked by Goldhammer corporate to lead the Los Angeles office. It was Miner who had chosen the Far East motif for the office, and Miner often quoted his favorite book, Sun Tzu's *Art of War*. After briefing everyone on the background of the airport, he would turn his attention to the competitors—us.

"There are three or four of the usual suspects involved," he would say. "But the wildcard is Greenberg Capital."

This name would be familiar to all of them—we were local, and occasionally, Goldhammer and Greenberg would cross paths.

Goldhammer's top pitch guy, Timothy Chance, would be quietly listening. He knew us and had worked with me for a few months in the 1990s. Since then, we had clashed several times. Three years ago, at a funding conference, Chance and I had exchanged words and had to be separated.

In the end, I imagined that Chance and Miner would look at each other, both knowing that this was the biggest pitch of the year—the one that bonuses would rest on. And it would be the one deal that would let the industry know who was best.

Strategy Sessions and Research

The first meeting at Greenberg Capital was a strategy session. Sam Greenberg, Rob McFarlen, and I sat in a conference room, and Greenberg delegated the various responsibilities. The pitch was a risk for all parties—the legal fees alone would be nearly $40,000. And the final bill for all the soft costs would be close to $100,000.

McFarlen and I began the long and arduous task of running numbers on the deal. McFarlen was a quantitative analyst, and he knew the types of financial models that were needed.

I had the role of putting together the big picture and the storyline—and I would be the one to actually make the presentation.

Greenberg would pay the bills and make sure that everything was tracking to his liking.

A few hours later, we took a break for lunch and started talking about Goldhammer.

"I'm wondering if they are gonna bring in Timothy Chance." Greenberg said.

"I hope so," I said. "He's the best they have, and the good news is that I know how his mind works."

"What do you think, Rob?" Greenberg asked.

McFarlen had a conflict of interest because he freelanced for Goldhammer as well. He shrugged. "My job is just to run numbers, not to pick sides."

"Go ahead. You can say it," I told him.

"Timothy is as good as they get," McFarlen said. "Superpolished. But I'm sure you are, too."

Greenberg watched me wince and smiled to himself. I'd taught him frame control, and now he was using it on me. Nice. This was typical Greenberg, always playing the game, trying to get people to work beyond their limits.

"You know what I think," I said. "If they do bring in Timothy, it will make things difficult. He's good."

We were making progress on the financing structure of the deal. We'd done research on comparable deals worldwide and felt that we had a good finance strategy in place with a track record to back it up.

We also confirmed that, indeed, Timothy Chance would be making the pitch on behalf of Goldhammer. This provided a jolt of adrenaline that helped me through the late nights of preparation.

Over the years, I'd been obsessed with putting together a method to the madness of presenting and closing deals. I'd developed the concept of neurofinance, perused scholarly journals, interviewed professors and researchers, and even set up experiments with executives to gauge their reactions to various pitching styles. However, all this research, as well as the 10,000 hours I spent on the subject, would do nobody any good unless it really worked. And it was clear that this $1 billion airport pitch would be the ultimate test of what I had learned and, if Greenberg Capital won, the ultimate confirmation of my methods.

Middle of January

The daily rhythm of work, the rhapsody of ticking things off the to-do list, the grind of crunching numbers—these things were giving me a sense of purpose and a daily jolt of exhilaration. I didn't tell Greenberg, but I'd been bored out there in the desert. Yeah, hot sand feels good on your toes, but if you're used to being a gunslinger, there's *nothing* like being in a live deal.

McFarlen had come over to my home to discuss the latest numbers, and I was explaining this very thing—the thrill of the deal.

"In a sense, it's very gladiator-oriented," I said. "You have to kill—or be killed. And if you do go down if you fail, the spectators, the people you're pitching, often experience perverse joy."

McFarlen nodded. I was always giving him vivid and clarifying metaphors, but McFarlen wasn't wired to really pay attention to all that. He was an introvert, who only broke out of quiet mode to defend his financial analysis. He was a numbers guy with a low-key personality.

"Who is Goldhammer using to run these numbers?" I asked. "If you know."

"They are doing it in-house, so it'll be Brandon Caldwell," McFarlen replied.

"Can he do what you do?" I asked.

"What do I do?" McFarlen wondered.

"You make magic out of the mundane," I said.

"No," McFarlen said. "Caldwell can't do ... what I do. Not with the short timeline." And this was the most bravado that I could pull out of McFarlen.

In McFarlen and me, Greenberg had indeed lined up two very skilled professionals. But Greenberg was no slouch either. He was a math whiz, and when I was just starting in the business, I looked up to Greenberg as my pitching mentor. This little team certainly had the talent and the experience. We just had a lot to overcome to bring the airport deal home.

The Client

Simon Jeffries owned the airport deal. He had worked for years to get all the pieces in place. Jeffries and Greenberg had known each other for more than a decade, and from time to time, they'd see each other in development circles. Now Jeffries was in an alpha status position. He was the guy who would hear the Goldhammer and Greenberg pitches and ultimately decide who would get a contract to raise $1 billion for the new airport.

Interestingly, while Chance was probably doing tons of research on Jeffries, I did none. I was not interested in building so-called deep rapport—a personal connection with my audience.

My research had shown that the small talk at the beginning of a pitch typically was fruitless. People who make million- and billion-dollar decisions don't care where you play golf or whether you had trouble finding a parking spot. I had learned this early on and avoided the deep-rapport trap that many pitchmen step into. I would be focused, instead, on a unique theme and storyline. A compelling human drama.

On paper, the proposed JetPark Airport is a beauty. A renowned architect had designed a 1,000-acre metropolis built around the famous Davis Field runway, which extends nearly 7,000 feet. The plans included restaurants, shopping, and amenities. Most of the buildings—now just renderings—would be multistory glass-and-steel monoliths. No detail had been spared.

The revamped airport was expected to help southern California deal with a staggering rise in air traffic (an estimated 30 million passengers will fly out of LAX in 2010 alone). The airport also would service smaller aircraft and provide quality office space for businesses that support the aviation industry. All told, the airport was expected to bring 10,000 jobs and and to have an economic impact of $2.2 billion.

Getting funding, therefore—this was serious business. Southern California *needed* the new airport. The new airport needed money. And both Greenberg and Goldhammer needed to win.

Nine Days Before the Big Pitch

McFarlen was working 16-hour days reconfiguring the deal structure. Today, I was working with a graphic designer on creating a visual "face-melter" to accompany my pitch. I wanted the visuals for the presentation to pop and shock.

I also was working on the elements of "the story." Some of my friends were Hollywood screenwriters, and they had beat it into me: *Every pitch should tell a story.*

"There's gotta be an intrigue hook," I told McFarlen. "If the shark in *Jaws* has a GPS beacon on it, and you know where it is all the time, then there's no drama, and the story is not interesting."

I was now reframing the entire campaign to include a human element. Sometimes deals are done strictly on numbers—but not this time. This time, it was about people.

McFarlen nodded and got back to his numbers.

The Day of the Pitch Arrives

At 2:52 p.m. on pitch day, I saw Tim Chance entering the building a few steps ahead of me. In the main building lobby, I went over the pitch again in my head. The plan was to focus on the Hollywood story aspect—to talk about the people I'd met in Spring Hill, the community where the airport was located. I felt certain that neither Tim Chance nor anyone else at his firm had ever set foot in Spring Hill before. As I made my way up the elevator to the ninth floor, I had a quiet confidence in my pitch strategy. The financial structure was solid, and Greenberg Capital had a strong track record to stand on, but the story I'd prepared had something stronger. A human angle that was compelling.

Simon Jeffries' office covers 3,000 square feet of prime Los Angeles office space. I walked into the reception area and saw Chance tapping out a text. We made eye contact, and I arched my eyebrows—my way of saying hello—and turned to the receptionist.

"The Greenberg team is here," I said, grinning.

"Go ahead and have a seat," she said.

There were six chairs in this beta-trapped lobby. Rather than sit, I tried to provoke Chance a little ("You texting headquarters for last minute advice?"), but he wasn't in the mood to talk. He knew this was frame control in action. Anything he said would be framed, deframed, reframed, and flipped.

"Good luck," Chance said, and looked back down at his iPhone.

Jeffries eventually entered the reception area and shook hands with me and then Chance.

"Okay, gentleman, come this way," he said.

He led us down a long hallway into a conference room.

"Have a seat," he said.

Chance and I exchanged an uneasy look.

Jeffries excused himself, and as soon as he was out of earshot, Chance said, "We're pitching in front of each other? You've gotta be kidding me."

Perfect. "This happens all the time," I said. "You should get out and pitch more."

What Jeffries probably knew was that if he listened to both of us pitch, on our terms, he'd get our rehearsed efforts. If he was going to trust either of us to raise $1 billion, he wanted to see how we reacted when things didn't go as planned.

Just then, a third pitchman entered. He was from a firm in London. This thing was going to be even more competitive than I'd anticipated.

Anatomy of a Pitch

Two months ago, I'd begun sizing up Goldhammer and wondering how I could get an advantage. Both teams would be working from the same information, so what would make the difference? It was a puzzle to solve, with the winner earning the opportunity to raise $1 billion and getting a $25 million payday.

Despite the stakes, I'd rewired my mind to think about it as "just another pitch" so I wouldn't feel all the pressure or do anything desperate when the moment came. Easy to say, but difficult to do. How do you spend weeks or months working on a big presentation and *not* be anxious about it? I had to invert my own psychology because, as human beings, we are all hardwired to be emotional about important social encounters. What worked for me were the three rules of *eradicating neediness*:

1. *Eliminate your desires.* It's not necessary to want things. Sometimes you have to let them come to you.
2. *Be excellent in the presence of others.* Show people one thing that you are very good at.
3. *Withdraw.* At a crucial moment, when people are expecting you to come after them, pull away.

If I could not eliminate my desire to win while preparing, then the team likely would seem needy and desperate on the day of the pitch. If I could not be excellent at pitching just one simple idea, then the competition would win because they were, on average, stronger. If I didn't have the nerve to withdraw at the right time, then I would just end up chasing the deal—and therefore losing it.

I knew that this had become a simple game involving the four pitch phases, and I should just have fun playing it. Toward that end, the first task for the team was to understand the mind-set of Simon Jeffries. I had to tune my pitch message to Jeffries' crocodile brain.

First, I had to hit the right tone. In fact, this would be a formal affair. Jeffries had been dealing with the Federal Aviation Administration (FAA) for several years. That experience surely would have set the "fun-dial" to low—these guys wouldn't be used to free-wheeling humor and high energy. Jeffries also was working with city, state, and federal agencies, so I would have to show a certain serious, respectful tone. But a "serious" tone, doesn't mean somber. Having fun with the pitch was absolutely critical. If the presentation isn't fun for the person giving it, then everyone else becomes anxious. And because there's no way to fake "having fun," I would really have to be enjoying myself. That in itself would eliminate desire.

Second, I had to get the frame right. This can be explained quite simply: The competition would make this about money and profits. They were sure to frame this deal as a "money-making opportunity." That's what they always did. What was being overlooked by these Wall Street types is that Simon Jeffries is not the head of just any old development company. He was head of a company that was about to redevelop one of the most historically significant airport runways in southern California. Jeffries would want to be known as the man who *saved* Davis Field when others couldn't. This redevelopment plan had been tried many times before—and failed. Jeffries would be building an airport on 1,000 acres of southern California land, land with a history dating back to the 1920s. This didn't have to be a deal about money. Instead, it could be about something bigger, something that tapped into the human desire to be the alpha in a social situation. The brain is wired to do things to achieve status, not money. And within that notion, the big idea was born. This deal was about *legacy*.

This deal was about building a legacy from a piece of American history. Simon Jeffries wanted to be remembered for doing something important. That is desire working, not greed. In this realization, the hard work was done. All I had to do was tune my pitch to this desire and be part of the plan by which Jefferies could secure his legacy.

Third, I had to hit the buttons that produce hot cognitions with a sledgehammer. All the hours logged on Sam Greenberg's plane had made an impression. Jets are intoxicating, plain and simple. They are pure hot cognition. Jeffries and the committee were deeply involved in the aviation business. They either owned planes or worked with them. Two were pilots themselves. When presenting to someone who loves jet aircraft, hitting hot buttons is almost too easy. You just show lots of visuals of jets.

Any product that your target consciously or subconsciously believes will enhance his social image *will get his brain hot with desire*. Show the brain something that society values, and you won't just be hitting hot buttons, you'll be *stomping on them*. Dopamine will pour into the reward structure of the brain, and the emotion of pleasure will rise fast. It's the same reward structure that's involved in the response to recreational drugs. When most people enter a social interaction that involves something like a Ferrari; a Rolex; beautiful ornaments; a Renoir, a Cezanne, a Titian, or a de Kooning; a pedigreed Rottweiler; a beachfront mansion; or as in this case, a private jet, their hot cognitions fire like crazy. They anticipate desire and rewards, and it feels good to them.

This is why I planned to show Jeffries and the committee large poster boards covered with "aviation porn." Every few minutes, I'd flip around a new posterboard—each with an increasingly provocative photo of a beautiful jet taking off, landing, or doing a high-bank turn.

In other presentations, when pitching derivatives or abstract financial instruments, it was much harder to hit the target's hot buttons visually, but with this deal, the jet narrative would make it *easy*.

I knew if I could just make it to the final selection, it would come down to Goldhammer and us. They had the deepest bench, the best track record, and the most influence. The inventory of their strengths was awesome. In the preceding 10 years, they had trounced us whenever they went after the same target. And there is no doubt that they would be discounting us because of our small size. I'd personally raised $400 million. But those guys? Goldhammer was doing billions.

As the presentation began to take shape, I built it around the four phases:

Phase 1: Frame control, grab status, introduce the big idea.
Phase 2: Explain the problem/solution and our special advantage.
Phase 3: Offer the deal.
Phase 4: Stack frames for hot cognition.

There was a deeper problem than just the competition. Simon Jeffries and the committee were natural alphas. During the pitch, they would be vocal, disruptive, and distracting. If I didn't seize the status and control the frame, these guys certainly would. At any point, if my pitch slowed to a crawl, they would jump in and try to assert their alpha status. They'd demand to know, "How do you plan to do that specifically?" or "Where'd you get those figures?" or "How much will such-and-such cost?"

To keep them out of this detective mode, I would need to constantly deploy push/pulls. This would keep them either rocked back on their heels or leaning forward and intrigued to know more. They wouldn't have time to become cold and analytical. They wouldn't be able to disrupt the frame. They would always be in *my* frame, reacting to *me*. I would have to seize star power status early.

Prepitch Thoughts

Here's what was running through my head at the last minute:

1. Get the tone right, frame myself as the alpha, seize status, and hit their hot buttons.
2. Deploy a big idea that is human and captures the theme of "building a legacy."
3. Keep it captivating with visuals that resonate.
4. Create hot cognitions. Make Jeffries and the committee *want* the idea before they even know the details.

The plan was to have a 20-minute high-temperature conversation with the targets' croc brains. The goal was to achieve a pitch full of hot cognitions. I believe that if two equally skilled people pitch the same idea and one tunes it to the neocortex and the other tunes it to the crocodile brain, you have two very different results. I had tuned my pitch for the targets' croc brains and was ready to start.

The Presentation

I'd been preparing for over two months, and now, with Chance watching, I stood up to address Jeffries and his committee. Speaking slowly, I began:

"There is a tremendous responsibility for all of us today. This is a decision not about who is the most charming or the most skilled in finance but instead about who has the *right ideas* that can raise $1 billion for Davis Field. Others have tried this kind of thing before and failed, so it's not that the best man should win or that the best team should win, but instead, the best ideas should triumph today. This runway has served the United States of America in World War II and hosted squadrons of B-17 bombers and other fighter planes that took part in the Pacific campaigns. Today, we are not talking about building a shopping center or strip mall or motel. We are building an airport, and we are doing it on hallowed ground. This has to be done right."

It was critical to get the frame right at the beginning. And because Goldhammer definitely would open by highlighting their size, experience, and track record, I had to pick a frame that minimized their strengths and focused the lens of attention on ours. This is why I chose the *best idea frame*. In other words, I was telling the targets that they should forget about picking a bidder with size and power. Instead, they should focus on the quality of ideas. We could not compete on size and power against the others, but if I changed the frame, if my big idea frame was stronger than Goldhammer's, then we could still win.

I'd also cranked up the tension, injecting norepinephrine into their brains by saying, "This is hallowed ground." In other words, a screw-up would have serious consequences.

If had I hit the tone just right, then a strong frame would be in place. The next task was to reframe the competition:

"We are honored to be competing against two other great firms today. I know each of them could serve you well because they have large teams, multiple offices, legions of young, energetic researchers, and the best-paid analysts in the world, and when working a deal, these firms spare no expense to tackle the job."

This was my way of saying that Goldhammer and the group from London were big, bloated corporations with too many people, many of them young and inexperienced. With this statement, I had reframed the competition as young, overstaffed, worried about their fees, and generally overweight. This fit the general image that dogged Wall Street banks in the media and would be an easy idea to convey. I knew that Goldhammer's Tim Chance would have to invest much of his precious time digging the company out of that frame. Chance recognized what I'd just done, and it's no wonder he was scowling. Things had started well for us.

"Simon, the vast majority of people you have met in the last three months have told you that the market is flat and that nothing has changed for some time. But if you start challenging the way these folks are thinking, you can start to see this market through a different lens—the lens we use. Let me explain. Three market forces that we follow very carefully have formed an important market window that we can step through—if we time it right. We don't think the window stays open for long, but if we do this now, we can go get $1 billion from investors faster than any other deal out there. Here's our analysis of the way markets are moving:

> "*Social factors*. Everyone is tired of investment bankers getting fat off these deals with no risk, so we have to be more transparent on fees.
> "*Economic factors*. For deals that are transparent, where the bankers and consultants are willing to risk alongside investors, there's a glut of investor money in the market now. $5 billion more than last quarter.
> "*Technology factors*. If we go green and make the buildings LEED-certified, I know a government agency that will get us a 10 percent reduction in taxes.

"I know this is news to you, but this is how the market is moving, and these three forces are important to our strategy. Again, we have a short market window to step through. If we fight against these forces, we will struggle. If we hit it right, though, we'll be one of the few deals that gets through this small market window."

This was the three-market-forces pattern that I had long endorsed. Simple and straightforward. I wasn't going to start selling and promoting before I was done framing. That would be a mistake. By doing it this way, I would show the targets how the market was moving. This would work because the mind is not a camera; it is a machine dedicated to observing motion and predicting what will happen next. I continued:

"Before going into my plan in any detail, let me tell you what we recognized some time ago. This project is more than an airport upgrade or an airport relaunch. *It is a legacy you will leave behind.* You will have your names written in history, and you we will be judged by generations to come by what you build here."

I had issued a challenge to the committee. Done this way, it creates a dopamine and norepinephrine kick at the same time. In other words, they would feel the twin pull of desire and tension.

"Simon, Jeff, Jim [I addressed the committee by their first names], I know you need to find investors for this airport as fast as possible, and I appreciate how questioning conventional wisdom is hard to do when time is tight. But today we are going to ask you to question how things have always been done because lately, the 'usual' way of doing these deals turns out to be wrong or wide off the mark or both.

"There are too many similar, me-too deals in this market. Right now, unless you are different in your approach from all the others, you will be wasting time and money.

"That's why our big idea is different from all the other plans, as you'll see.

[I flipped around a few big posterboards with the theme and logotype boldly printed.]

"As you can see, our theme is 'Invest in an American Legacy.'

"Our plan gives plenty of profit to investors but also gives them a chance to be part of an amazing story. Unlike the other bidders here today, who will just be telling the potential investors a profit-and-loss story, we plan to tell the investors a wonderful story about an airport that has a rich aviation history.

"The combination of the 'American Legacy' theme with our financial plan will work best in the market. Our approach will raise $1 billion faster and more easily. Our big idea delivers a better velocity of capital and more certainty that you will get the money you need. We are going to set our sights high, to literally become heroes by protecting—not destroying—a piece of aviation history and get $1 billion at the same time."

This was my classic *big idea introduction pattern*. Why would this kind of introduction for the big idea work here? There are three basic truths about the brain and decision making that went into it. *First,* the most basic working principle of the brain is: Decisions of *wanting something* are not conscious. *Second,* the opportunity to gain a social reward, such as becoming a "hero," is *even more enticing than making money. Third,* you can flood the target's brain with dopamine by focusing on three ideas: (1) the idea of social rewards, (2) the idea of becoming a "hero," and (3) the idea of making a lot of money. The purpose? Ignite desire.

Now, at this point of the pitch, I'd served the committee's crocodile brains the right cocktail of dopamine (desire) and norepinephrine (tension), and I was free to proceed with the boring stuff: the numbers.

By creating a frame that focused the attention of the targets on what we were good at, I'd put some distance between ourselves and Goldhammer. Being different also creates novelty. And that gets the dopamine injectors in the brain flowing. Traditional pitches often start out, "We worked really hard to come up with a great plan. ..."

But my approach takes two steps back and then goes three steps forward. It begins by saying: "Things have changed out there in the market [and the normal approach isn't going to work]," and it ends up by saying, "There is a better way that is different from the others," and "It's different because it isn't just cold, hard numbers. It has a human story to it."

The other groups probably would do precisely the wrong thing: Focus a huge amount of time on their wonderful résumés. They would all be using the same theme, only the details would be different, relying on clichés, framing themselves as a "full-service firm" that caters to clients and provides the "highest levels of integrity, service, and quality." There is nothing gained with that old, ineffective way, so why waste the time? Doesn't everyone just assume that you're going to provide service and quality?

Over the next five minutes, I gave highlights of the budget and what timeline I could deliver on. If I could not pitch the full plan in five minutes, then the last two months would become a very expensive waste of time and money.

In preparing for this day, the difficulty was knowing what to take out of the pitch without stripping away the richness and complexity of the idea. But I felt that I would have a better chance of success with fewer cold, hard details, the kind that switch the brains of the targets into analytical mode.

The length of the Pitch also was of paramount importance. During a rehearsal a month earlier, the pitch came in at more than

55 minutes. Too long. So I started hacking. I edited three minutes from the total, then another two minutes, and so on. With each new rehearsal, I removed details that lacked intrigue or hot cognition. As recently as one week before the presentation, I was still working on making the pitch hotter, shaving away distracting details while keeping the core message.

So now, here I was, pushing through the budget and the financing details in about five minutes. It was the coldest part of the pitch. Soon, I would deliver the *four-frame hot cognition stack*—which would heat things up. But first a quick push/pull:

"Is this plan bold? Well, we can certainly debate if my numbers are 5 percent too high or 3 percent too low, but there is no doubt the big idea *is* bold. We think that boldness is important. And if you don't like bold plans, then there's a real possibility that we are not right for each other because my team would always be working quickly in an entrepreneurial way, and you always would be responding like a big corporation—slow and methodical. And how could that ever work? So I'm okay with the notion that our plan is too bold and that we aren't right for each other."

I was employing the classic push part of the push/pull pattern, which challenged the targets and amplified tension. Now it was time to back off. I had a lot going on here, drawing on the techniques and research that had consumed me for more than a decade. No matter what kind of soft touch I had, this was still a form of selling, I was trying to get the targets to decide in my favor, trying to take control. And to my targets, this was a form of stress and pressure. Humans behave a certain way when they are put under this kind of pressure. At a basic level, in a target's croc brain, there's a feeling that you are taking away his or her automony. A threat response could be triggered.

The push would counter this problem, giving the targets the opportunity to make a pressure-free decision.

Because the human brain evolved in response to stressors over thousands of years, humans are constantly attuned, at the level of the croc brain, to the ways social encounters threaten their capacity for choice. This is one of my guiding theories: The slightest perception that you are taking away free will (scientists call this *reducing the autonomy of choice*) will trigger a threat response.

After letting the croc brain know that it didn't have its back against the wall, it was time to complete the other half of the push/pull pattern:

"But then again, if this did work out, our forces could combine to become something great. Imagine, your aviation experience and passion combined with our strategy and financial know-how. Almost like some kind of superpower, when we focus our gaze on any individual investor, he would just explode with desire!"

I then returned to the idea of status. The brain is always assessing how social encounters either enhance or diminish its status. Yet, at this point, all the competitors had higher global status than we did. There was no way around that. They had more wealth, more popularity, and more power—the three measures of status. So I needed some local star power, and I needed it fast.

"Look, in all seriousness, we love this project."

I started flipping over heavy posterboards that were set around the room. These were big, physical, real-world boards, about $1/2$ inch thick each. Unlike a PowerPoint slide, which would just disappear, these would remain, adding a certain concrete feeling of reality to the whole pitch.

"And I know how difficult it is not to choose Goldhammer or the London team, sitting here with us. How great are those guys? Is there anything they can't do with all that youthful energy and those amazing bespoke suits? But one thing I would have to ask them: How much do they know about Spring Hill pickup football?"

This was a novelty play that would keep attention high. But it was risky, because if you are going to go off on a tangent—it had better be good.

"There's a reason I ask, because the full story of Davis Field and why the previous attempts to build a new airport here failed cannot be fully told until you meet Joe Ramirez."

I had indeed met an auto mechanic named Joe Ramirez while doing my research on the airport deal. He was tall, with wavy hair and a prematurely graying goatee. Now, here he was, striding across the room dressed as if he was going to church. You can imagine how a mechanic would have been received by the committee, in the middle of a pitch for a $1 billion contract. Nobody expected this. Clearly, he was not here to explain financial plans or flight intervals. I urged him to take his time and speak from the heart.

The clock was ticking, but this moment was too rich to be rushed. Joe moved in front of the lectern and pulled from his pocket a folded piece of notebook paper. He read aloud his prepared comments:

"I grew up in Spring Hill. It's been my home since my father came here from Dallas, Texas. As a kid, there wasn't much to do. We didn't have the mall and the theaters and the skateboard park. But what we did have was a football field. It was at the airport, here [he pointed to a place on the map, just adjacent the runway]. Every Saturday and Sunday we played football there. Two or three games would be going all the time. This place was easy for everyone to get to, and some of my best memories growing up happened right here. But in 1997, nobody knows why, the city paved the field. It's been an empty parking lot since that day. If there's anything you can do. ..."

You could clearly see the emotion in Joe's face; you'd have to have been either a robot or from an alien planet not to be moved yourself. When Joe said that the city had paved his football field into an unused parking lot, there was a certain heaviness in the room.

Heightened states of emotion create strong memories. *Where were you when such-and-such famous person died?* It's easy to remember. The parts of the brain where memories are stored needs to distinguish between significant experiences and those which carry less importance. This was one such moment. While it is hard to define emotion specifically, what is not hard is to show its effect on cognition and decision making. Emotions are how we encode things of value and how we link events to our memory. If it is true that emotional intensity creates a moment where attention is high and encoding is high and where desire could be created, *I would not get a better opportunity to create "wanting" from the committee.*

I thanked Ramirez and stepped back to the front of the room.

"Simon, committee ... You see, we can look at the numbers behind this deal all day long: 24 percent of this, 15 percent of that, $100 million for solar panels, $100 million for construction of just one terminal. One billion dollars. It's all just numbers. We have all been thinking of this airport as if it is a purely financial transaction. As if this is a 7,000-foot runway in some kind of cyberspace. What I realized just 30 days ago, and what has been forgotten in all our desire to design it and build it and profit from it, is that this airport isn't in cyberspace and it's no longer 1948 when this runway was in the middle of nowhere. What I'm saying is, 50 years ago, Spring Hill was populated by fewer than 1,000 people, who were probably outnumbered by the jackrabbits. Now, 115,000 people live here. Think about that. We are deciding in this room, 50 miles away from the site, what will be done with 1,000 acres of land in the middle of a community."

With this, I put the morality frame into play. It would be hard for the other groups to find a higher set of values to champion than protecting a community of more than 100,000 souls. This frame is so basic, so tied to the workings of the social animal, that it had to be deployed. This was the right moment. Next, the time frame would be used:

"I have to finish in five minutes, so I don't have the time right now to introduce you to the 37 other friends of mine who live in Spring Hill. You see, I've been living there for the last few weeks in a cool little hotel on Main and 19th Street. I've played pickup football in a dirt field outside town. That's where I met Joe. So I can tell you that this is an amazing community that will support us if we play fair and support them as well."

Emotion in the room was peaking.

Simon Jeffries couldn't hold off any longer. He was already leaning forward in his seat almost past the edge. "You lived there? You know all these people?" Jeffries asked. What had been a formal pitch was now becoming a casual conversation. "They're your friends, and you know their names?"

"I'm good with names," I said. "And those people all had something important to say about this project."

"This is why our plan includes an athletic park to return to Joe and the community the football field he loved so much growing up. We also want a young aviators' center added to the build. With $1 billion, this is a rich project, and we can afford it. We'll pay for it ourselves. Here are the plans."

I flipped around another posterboard. Now it was becoming like a game show.

"Are you sure that you want to commit to these things?" Jeffries asked.

"How can we *not* do it?" I said. "You can't just pull value out of a community. You have to put value back in."

Following the principles of seized status, I would now redistribute some of the alpha status and frame control I was holding to some of the other players:

"And the park plans with the restoration of the historic football field are complete. They're not just part of my theory. These are real plans. We completed the engineering specifications, and I want them to be part of any plan that goes forward. Five minutes ago we e-mailed these plans to everyone in this room. No matter what happens with our bid, whether you choose us or not, we want the football field to be restored."

I flipped around the final display boards with their beautiful, evocative visuals of aircraft overhead and kids playing football and proud community members holding their arms in an open embrace. These were all big-picture visuals meant to stoke the fires of hot cognitions. For a closing statement, I would bring it all together. *Time frame. Prize frame. Intrigue. Morality frame. Push. Pull. Desire. Tension.* It was a fireworks finale of frame collisions:

"Committee, the only thing worse than an idea you hate is an idea you just 'like.' When you only 'like' an idea, then you are still unsure about it. Imagine getting married to someone you only 'liked.' It would seem cold. If I were sitting where you are, what would be important to me? I might think, if we don't love this idea of 'American Legacy,' then we have to throw these guys out of here right now.

"And that would be okay with me because it would be the right thing to do. And by the same measure, if you only 'like' us, then you also must throw us out. And I'm totally okay with that, too. Because we could not possible work with you if you didn't love our big idea. We believe in the big idea that strongly.

"Right now, as we are sitting here, the terminal paint at Davis Field is peeling, the old observation deck is rotting, and a local park has been paved over. Almost everything about Davis Field Municipal Airport shows age and neglect. It is a place that by almost every appearance has been left behind in time.

"But time should not leave this place behind. The war in the Pacific was fought from this field. Bomber squadrons had thousands of movements here. Men left this field to fight for our country, and for some, it was the last patch of American soil they ever touched.

"So if you love the idea of an American Legacy and you want Joe Ramirez's kids to be able to play on that field, and you want to be known as the capitalists who built a legacy for the ages, then we are the right team to pick today because we know how to do this better than anyone else. But we are not going to do this *for* you. We will have to do it *together* with you. When you feel that the time is right, *I encourage you to come to our office and talk over how we can make that happen.*"

The prize frame can be boiled down to one thing: Withdrawal. At a crucial moment, when the committee was expecting me to come after them, I pulled away.

I remembered what was once written in the *US Air Force Training Manual*, "It is generally inadvisable to eject directly over the area you have just bombed." Strictly following that advice, it was time to leave.

In the course of my many pitches, I discovered that people won't do what you tell them to. They must feel as if they have free will to make their own decisions. They won't even know what to do unless you have created primary basic and inescapable emotions for them to react to. They can't encode your pitch into their memory without strong rushes of dopamine and norepinephrine, resulting in the twin forces of desire and tension.

In that moment, everyone realized that Greenberg's little company of six people (plus seven consultants) had a chance to win against the biggest and best in the financial industry. I had built from scratch a pitch that worked in a market where nothing worked. That's when I realized that this was the most exciting 20 minutes in my career of pitching deals.

The Competition Strikes Back

Tim Chance was up next, and as expected, his presentation was polished, practiced, and predictable. He opened with a long explanation of the many large deals his firm, Goldhammer, had done in recent years, the amazing capability of his organization, and the respected name it held. The logo on his business card was known around the world, and he was using it to his best advantage.

There was a moment of unintentional comedy right away: While Tim was making his opening remarks, his team was fumbling with the laptop they had brought, trying to connect it to the conference room projector. Although we've all seen this happen before—it still makes me laugh. With all that was at stake—*how could they burn five minutes this way?* We had worked for *two days* to cut just *three minutes* from our presentation. My question was soon answered: As his slide deck came into focus, I and several others in the room noticed the little number in the lower right corner of the screen: 42. Oh boy! There were 42 slides in his presentation. *This was going to take a while.*

After the review of Goldhammer's bona fides, information we all knew anyway, Chance launched into a lengthy and detailed opinion of current market conditions. I could feel the temperature of the room falling toward subzero as the cold cognitions he was flashing on the screen were sending our brains into a deep freeze. While he certainly looked good and sounded good from the podium, he was talking about data and not about what really mattered, which should have been Why now? How? and the critical path for doing it.

Chance was banking on a tried-and-true method that Goliath-sized companies often use. Because they're big and successful, they think that it implies that they are also capable, and therefore, they often do not speak directly to how they will accomplish an objective. They believe that their audience assumes "it will get done," but *will it really?* We are left to wonder. In large companies, deal makers like Chance are rewarded for the business they bring to their firms, not necessarily the results.

Each of us had been granted up to one hour to present, and unbelievably, Chance used every minute he was allotted. After 40 minutes of this financial mumbo-jumbo, he was inducing a coma in me. Tim was the only member of his team to speak, and he dragged the audience through every single one of the words in every single one of his densely worded slides. *This is doing them no favors*, I thought, but it's good for me.

Next up was the team from London, who, *mercifully*, did not speak for an hour. On the contrary, their presentation was the model of European efficiency—clean, slick, and heavy with emphasis on financial models. This team had the "Wow factor" on their side, too, using an animated three-dimensional digital presentation of their previous aviation projects. I was impressed. They had more experience in aviation than the rest of us combined.

Like Goldhammer, they eventually succumbed to the temptation every presenter faces: taking a deep dive into complicated financial figures, and as their team commented on how they would manage the deal, it became clear that this was merely production work to them—no different than any other airport project they've ever worked on. If awarded, they'd stamp this project out cookie-cutter style. They expressed no interest in the local community and seemed to have no concern with the economic impact. They focused only on the project funding—how quickly they could get in, get it done, and get out.

I could not help but be impressed by their confidence and felt certain that they could do this deal—and do a great job. These guys could win it easily.

As they finished with a rich European flourish—puffed chests, thick Oxford accents, and broad smiles—the last thing they said was, "So we would be proud to work on this prestigious project and will eagerly wait to hear your decision."

Beta trapped! After all that work, showing neediness was the wrong move. Simon Jeffries approached the podium to make some final remarks. Simon is a class act. He graciously thanked the teams for their presentations, described the week-long deliberation process he would now preside over, and quickly brought the meeting to a close.

The Hour of Judgment

After it was all said and done, I sat there, looking out the window of Greenberg's Los Angeles office. There were five others with me, waiting for a phone call. *The* phone call. Jeffries, meanwhile, had gathered several members of his selection committee at his office, presumably to discuss last-minute details.

As I looked out at Los Angeles, I reflected on the last few months, this pitch, and its repercussions. I'd boiled down two months of work into a lean and elegant pitch lasting 20 minutes and 52 seconds. Now it would all came down to this call. This moment. The decision. The phone rang. I sat down at the table in the conference room, and Jeffries was put on speaker.

Jeffries began, "If you go down to Davis Field right now, as you pointed out to me, the terminal paint has worn off and the old observation deck is just rotting away. Almost everything has a hole in it, including important parts of the runway. Who would want to land a jet there, have it serviced there, or take a meeting there? Nobody." This was becoming melodramatic. We just wanted *the decision*.

"This is why I am so passionate about the new Davis Field and excited about building a new entrance to the airport and all new facilities. This can be one of the best private airports in the world. But I have got to pick the right team. The Greenberg team was fantastic in last week's pitch. There were some things that we felt you didn't get right, but we really enjoyed it. This is a hard decision, and of course, we can only pick one winner. . . ."

Jeffries let the moment linger for a torturous amount of time, and then he cleared his throat and said the word, "*Congratulations!*"

The office erupted into celebration.

For me, this journey back from the desert was complete, and my methods were validated. They weren't just a personal collection of pitching notes stuffed in my notebooks. It wasn't just thousands of index cards in my office. It wasn't just a bunch of academic notions or theories. And it wasn't just a checklist of dos and don'ts. Much in the way that calculus is a system for solving math problems, or civil engineering is a system for building bridges, my STRONG method was now a system to get deals done, especially when the stakes are high. It worked.

Chapter 8

Get in the Game

Learning to manage social dynamics is not an intuitive under-taking. Ten years ago, I found myself in many situations where I was the beta. I thought I had to accept this low social status and thought that there was almost nothing I could do to control the frame. I didn't even know what a frame was. And I cannot rationally describe to you why in those early days I disliked—even hated—traditional sales techniques.

I just knew what I wanted—a method that requires no blunt-force trauma. No beg-or-bash modalities that aggravate people and make them regret doing business with you. I wanted nothing to do with the anxiety and fear that accompany those beta-trapped, pushy methods.

Beta methods do not exist in my approach for the simple reason that you are not pushing—you are *interacting* with people using basic rules of social dynamics.

For years I've been doing this stuff around the country and the world, and part of what I've learned is that the crocodile brain is the same everywhere. There aren't New York croc brains and California editions and special French ones. Every croc brain responds the same:

- When something is boring: Ignore it.
- When something seems dangerous: Fight/run.
- When something is complicated: Radically summarize (causing information loss) and pass it on in severely truncated form.

With my approach, you are respecting the croc brain by introducing a game, and you are inviting others to play with you. It will feel new and different to everyone involved—because *it is.* Instead of flogging people with canned responses and pressure tactics, frame-based interactions excite the senses and engage people in a much more social way. In a world of robotic sameness, this approach will distinguish you from others.

I learned this alone, and it took me more than 10,000 hours of trial and error (and many patient and forgiving clients) to get it right. In the beginning, I seriously screwed up some important deals. I should have worked with a partner or a small group, but everyone I talked to about my method was afraid of it. Most thought it was chaotic and unpredictable because I didn't have the model worked out at that point. Today, the method isn't chaotic or unpredictable at all. Frames are now easy to control, and local star power can be created in every situation.

In the most basic sense, what are the frames I have been talking about here? Frames are psychological referencing systems that all people use to gain a perspective and relevance on issues. Frames influence judgment. Frames change the meaning of human behavior. If a friend rapidly closes and opens her eyes, we will respond differently depending on whether we think this is a physical frame (she blinked) or a social frame (she winked). Consider the words: *hit, bumped, collided,* and *smashed*. These words tell you the severity of an automobile accident. *Frames shape the underlying meaning of every social interaction.*

It is true, for instance, when we get together for a presentation, meeting, or pitch, that we can't just conduct a wholesale drop and transfer of information. You don't send a cargo container full of information to your customers or potential investors and say, "Here, look through this stuff. See what you can make out of it." They can't absorb it, and if they could, they don't have the time. This is a part of the presenter's problem: Deciding what to pitch and how is not like a math or engineering problem that can be worked out by having more and more information. It's about figuring out what parts of the information to use—which parts of your deal will trigger cold, analytical processing by the neocortex and which parts will engage the hot and vibrant processes of the crocodile brain.

This is exactly why frame control is so crucial. It serves to filter information and provide meaning, bridging the natural disconnect between the you and the target. It is always the case that frames can simplify complex issues by putting greater emphasis on one interpretation over others. In the process, frames construct a point of view.

And when you set the frame correctly, you control the agenda, which, of course, is important to do because every situation can be seen from many different angles. Frame control is about controlling which angle your deal is seen *from*. A frame helps to package a deal in a way that encourages certain interpretations and discourages others.

For instance, during the 1984 presidential campaign, there was considerable concern about Ronald Reagan's age. Speaking during the presidential debate with Walter Mondale, Reagan said, "I will not make age an issue of this campaign. I am not going to exploit, for political purposes, my opponent's youth and inexperience."

In one sense, this was a beautiful example of frame control in action. Reagan changed the underlying meaning of the social encounter and seized the alpha status, building a strong, unassailable point of view for the rest of the audience to follow and get behind. There is a second and equally valuable lesson from this example, and perhaps it is the critical learning of social dynamics: Humor, fun, and light-heartedness are crucial components of every pitch.

As I discussed in Chapter 1, in recent years I finally *got* the fundamental problem you and I have when we pitch something. We have our highly evolved neocortex, which is full of details and abstract concepts, trying to persuade the croc brain, which is afraid of almost everything and needs very simple, clear, direct, and non-threatening ideas, to decide in our favor. This realization guided me into the world of frames and status.

Since the beginning of this book, I have offered you two principal insights into social dynamics. The first is structural—you have to package ideas for the croc brain in such a way that you are generating *hot cognitions*. In other words, you avoid the kind of cold analysis that is done by the neocortex. Instead, you use visual and emotional stimuli to push your target's primal hot buttons—to create *wanting*.

The second insight is procedural: You always have to be on the watch for opposing power frames and then win the ensuing frame collisions with better, stronger frames. And then you must further your frame control by perpetrating small denials and showing defiance.

But now, there's a third element that I believe is fundamental to successful frame control, to seizing alpha status, and to social dynamics in general: *humor and having fun*.

Certainly, the purpose of perpetrating denials and defiance is to reframe social situations and to prize—that perhaps you aren't really selling them but that *they need to sell you*, that your own time is even *more valuable than theirs*, that under the circumstances, if they try to beta-trap you, you're *willing to withdraw*, that you aren't automatically willing to take the beta position you're being led into. *But in all this you must use humor as well.*

Importantly, the humor is not there to *relieve* tension. Instead, it's there to signal that although the tension is real, you are so confident that you can play around a little. Perhaps it's best to think about it this way: People who have lots of options are not uptight, and they don't take themselves too seriously.

It also signals that framing is a game, and it invites others to join in. If you take the power frame from a "master of the universe" and he or she takes it back from you, is that not a challenge to improve your game? If you talk to *frame masters*, they'll tell you that the secret of success is to create tension in a fun way that invites people to join in the frame game.

I mention this because most buyers/customers/investors will try to use the power frame on you. You'll see it frequently. Don't worry. It's a clumsy frame that is easy to disrupt using power-busting, intrigue, prizing, and time frames.

As easy as the power frame is for *you* to break, absorb, and control, many others can't, so buyers will be shell-shocked. Take it easy on them, and don't take advantage. In the buyer's experience, most salespeople submit to their every whim and command: *Meet me at such-and-such inconvenient place; wait for me; start now; no, wait, stop; do this; send me more info;* and so on. Once they come across someone like you who doesn't submit to these whims, they take notice, thinking, *This person is interesting. He isn't falling over himself to impress me like all the others. What's going on here?*

It's one thing to acknowledge the power of frames and seizing status but quite another to put the method to use. Becoming a frame master isn't easy. It takes thought, effort, and will, but the rewards are substantial. The good news—this is a journey that is fun from the very start, and if you are doing it right, it remains fun. In fact, if at any point you find that you are not having fun, something has gone wrong. Get with a colleague or friend who also knows this stuff and backtrack. See where the train hopped the tracks. I've had to do this many times. It's humbling, but what's the alternative? Go back to common industry practices like "interview the customer" and "trial closing"?

There is another benefit to becoming a frame master that isn't immediately apparent but will make a remarkable difference in your life. Over time, you will begin to notice an increase in the velocity of your work and leisure activities. This is so because strong frames allow you to selectively ignore things that do not move you forward toward your goals, and such a recognition amplifies your focus on the things that do.

In a natural way, framing keeps you focused on what is most important—human relationships—and prevents you from becoming distracted or burdened by unimportant matters when you are in social situations. Weak frames and nonessential details bounce off strong frames. Your abilities to discern, judge, decide, and act will vastly improve because the frame guides you.

Throughout this book I have talked about the structure of frames and the methods of seizing status. But mastery comes from actually doing it. This book will serve as your guide for a while, but as soon as you can, leave it behind. Your skills will come from practice, not from being a desk jockey, reading, or browsing the Internet for more learning. And I'm going to insist that you learn this stuff with a colleague or with a group because, as I said before, *learning to manage social dynamics is not an intuitive undertaking.*

Fortunately, frame control method comes naturally for most people who can follow the blueprint here and have a good sense of humor and a positive outlook on life. If this describes you, you should have no difficulty getting started.

Getting Started

When somebody wants to learn frames, social dynamics, and the overall method from me, I always begin with this warning: Frame-based social dynamics is strong medicine. Instead of reciting the same old business clichés that your audience expects to hear, you are jacking into the wetware that controls their brains, their primordial programming. You are simultaneously communicating with them on the surface and below the surface of their consciousness. If you do it wrong, for example, without humor, poise, and grace, I guarantee that security will be called, and you will be escorted from the building. I don't want to receive an angry e-mail from you telling me that you've just been fired, so please pay attention to the advice I'm about to give you.

Here are the progressive steps to learning the method:

Step 1: Learn to recognize beta traps and how to step around them. This is a low-risk way to train your mind to begin thinking in a frame-based way. As you go about the business of life, look for the beta traps. Identify anything that is designed to control your behavior, and think of how you would step around it. The key at this stage is to get good at seeing the traps (they are everywhere).

While there is no immediate harm in doing nothing, when you are told to wait in the lobby until called, it's a test. Remind yourself that if you step into this beta trap, the next one will be even larger and more difficult to overcome.

Step 2: In a gradual way, start stepping around beta traps. It will feel uncomfortable at first, of course, but it will push you forward to the place where it becomes natural and hardly noticeable to you. Work with a partner to practice beta-trap avoidance.

As I said at the start of this book, this method is powered by its simplicity. I've been practicing it for over 10 years, and I've survived and prospered using only four basic frames and the ability to avoid beta traps. So don't overcomplicate this or worry over your lack of technique. It will come naturally to you. Just be sure to have fun at it—that's the secret to success.

Step 3: Identify and label social frames. Notice the frames that are coming at you on every level of your life. Power frames, time frames, and analyst frames are everywhere, and they crash into you on a daily basis. Develop your ability to see them coming, describe them, and discuss them with your partner. Become very good at identifying frames using the unique language of framing.

Step 4: Begin to initiate frame collisions with safe targets— those who pose no major career risk to you. What I'm saying is, tomorrow, don't stride into the CEO's office, grab a sandwich out of his hand, and put your feet up on his desk, telling him that it's time you and he had a talk about your bonus.

Working with a partner, begin to overtake opposing frames in a fun, light-hearted way. I'm repeating this because it's so critical: Remember that humor and a soft touch are absolutely necessary. Without it, you will appear rude and arrogant and will trigger croc brain defense responses instead of engaging your target in a fun and spirited social exchange.

Step 5: The small acts of defiance and denial you use to take control of a social frame create a certain amount of conflict and tension. This is the point. Push. Pull. Delivering these acts with a soft touch reassures the target's croc brain that everything is okay—that there is no clear and present danger. If you are having difficulty at this stage, it is because you are triggering defensive responses, which means you are coming on too strong. If this is the case, *pause.* Do not press forward if you are struggling because that means that something is wrong. Find another partner to do this with, choose a different social environment, practice in another venue, or just punch "Reset" and start over.

Step 6: Frame control cannot be forced because this takes the fun out of it. This is not theater for someone else to enjoy. It's not a dog and pony show. It's a game for your own personal enjoyment—and for a moment, consider why we play games—to enjoy ourselves in a challenging but fair way where we can rack up a win.

If you find yourself forcing the method, fortunately, this is an easy problem to fix. Simply lighten up a little. When you say something that causes a frame collision, do it with a twinkle in your eye and a smile in your heart. Your target will feel your good will and good humor and respond in a positive way.

Above all, remember that this is not a conventional sales technique. You need not be a back-slapping, guffawing blow-hard to win business from your customers. There is no pressure here, no brute force, and no anxiety. Instead, this is a fun game that you bring to every target with whom you meet. Simply enjoy every moment, and others will enjoy it with you. It's nice to know that your continued happiness is what will make you successful. What could be easier?

Step 7: Work with other frame masters. Now that you have developed a basic level of skill, seek out others who are better than you. As with any other artistic or athletic endeavor, apprenticeship leads to mastery faster than going it alone. Continue to work with others. Like a 10th dan black belt, you never stop refining your technique and honing your mastery. Keep it simple, stick to a few frames that work for you, and avoid complication.

When you become a frame master—and even on your journey to becoming one—you will have the most fun you've ever had. I find myself cracking up sometimes in the middle of a pitch, even when the business I'm doing involves millions of dollars. Why not? *This is a game where you set the rules and then change the rules as needed to maintain your continuous advantage without ever upsetting your opponent.* Imagine that.

The only rule is that you make the rules that the others follow. Because you set the agenda and control the frame, this is a game you can never lose. How could that not be fun?

Most of the difficulties I've encountered in learning this method came from the fact that there was no common language to discuss these methods with people. Instead of saying, "Watch out! Here comes a power frame. We need to use strong moral authority and a power-busting frame to win this frame collision," I had to use long explanations, and in so doing, the moment and the opportunity were lost. This is why it's important to learn and use the *lingua franca* of frame control. Future conversations with your partner or group should sound like this:

"These guys set beta traps from the lobby all the way to the conference room. You have to time frame them immediately and withdraw. After that, they just hit you with power frames. Just break it with a prize frame. And then frame stack a few push/pull patterns."

Or, "Here comes the analyst frame. Let's hard-core intrigue frame, seize local star power, and withdraw."

Pitch Anything gives you a common vocabulary that will deepen your mastery of the method and ingrain frame-based thinking into your DNA. Here are the most important terms for you to know and to own personally:

Frame control
Power-busting frame
Frame collisions
Prizing
Beta traps
Seizing status
Local star power
Push/pull
Alpha
Hot cognition
Crocodile brain
Neocortex

These terms label the social phenomena that are invisible to others and that used to be invisible to you.

As you advance in your life and career, the challenges you will face will increase in proportion to the responsibilities you bear. Being a frame master will make those burdens seem lighter, will help others to see you as a sage and trusted leader, and will maintain your social value at a much higher level, even when you are not consciously practicing frame control.

By helping others to view situations and opportunities through your frame, it will make interacting with you seem effortless. It's easy for others to spend time with a person they agree with, in any setting, and that's how they will feel about you.

So go forth, learn frame control, practice it at every opportunity, and have fun doing so. I wish you much success, and I hope that it serves you as well as it continues to serve me. I invite you to learn more about frame control at pitchanything.net.

Index

Abstract concepts, 9, 139
Adrenaline, 107
Adrenaline rush, 172
Adventure, 169
"Aha" moment, 16, 17
Airport deal. *See* Case study (airport deal)
Alchemy of Finance, The (Soros), 131
Alpha, 77, 78
Always be closing (ABC), 67
Always be leaving (ABL), 67
Amygdala, 13
Analog human narratives, 140
Analyst frame, 44, 51, 52, 60
Analyst frame disruption, 56–57, 60–61
Analytical tangent, 67
Anger, 56
Anxiety, 107
Apprenticeship, 216
Attention, 49–50, 113
Attention getting, 112–116
Austin, Steve *(Six Million Dollar Man)*, 167
Avocado farmer's money, 41–48

Backstory, 100
Badgering, 62
"Being nice," 69
Bell, Gordon, 124
Belzberg, Bill, 19–20
Berns, Greg, 114
Best idea frame, 191
Beta trap, 78–84, 162, 213
Beta-trap avoidance, 214
Bifurcation, 121
Big idea introduction pattern, 194
Body language, 54
Boeing, 97
Brain
   abstract concepts, 139
   amygdala, 13
   basic truths, 194
   cognitive, as miser, 55, 112
   croc. *See* Crocodile (croc) brain
   decision making, 131
   development of, 8
   fundamental organizing principle, 107
   how it functions, 9, 12–14, 154
   memories, 199
   movement, 102, 103

Brain (*Cont.*)
  narrative and analytical infor-
    mation, 55
  narratives, 140
  neocortex, 8, 9, 111, 154, 210
  parts, 8
  pleasurable challenges, 54
  probabilities, 111
  scarcity bias, 147
  threat-avoidance system, 107
  threat responses, 108
"Brain is like a computer"
    metaphor, 10
"Brain Scanners Can *See* Your
    Decisions Before You Make
    Them," 131
Browbeat, 62
Bruner, Jerome, 132, 139
Budget, 124, 125
Building rapport, 77

Cardiac surgeon and golf pro,
    84–85
Case study (airport deal),
    171–206
  American Legacy theme, 194
  best idea frame, 191
  beta trap, 205
  big idea introduction
    pattern, 194
  competition (Goldhammer),
    178–179
  competitor's pitch,
    203–205
  eradicating neediness, 186
  hour of judgment, 205–206
  how to pitch, 187–188
  Klaff accepts to come on
    board, 175–178

  length of the pitch, 195–196,
    205
  prepitch thoughts, 190
  presentation, phases, 189
  push/pull, 196–197
  strategy sessions and research,
    180–181
  three-market-forces pattern,
    192–193
Change blindness, 102–103
Chase Manhattan, 134
Checking out, 54, 55
Chemical of alertness, 116
Chocolate vs. spinach, 153
Coffee shops, 81
Cognitive functioning, 132
Cold, reasoned analysis, 130,
    132, 133
Cold cognitions, 52, 155
Comedian (Seinfeld), 126
Competition, 125
Competitive advantage (secret
    sauce), 125–127
Complexity, 111
Conference room, 80
Conflict, 118, 122
Convention floor, 82
Conviction, 146
Cop frame, 25–26
Crick, Francis, 95
Crocodile (croc) brain, 8, 210.
    See also Brain
  basic rules, 208
  characteristics, 15–16
  choice, 197
  detailed explanation, 110
  filtering system, 11–12
  rubber mallet, 154
  self-protection, 160–161

survival, 9, 15
Curiosity, 116
Cymbalista, Flavia, 131, 132

Death match, 22
Defaulted debt, 133–136
Deframing, 3
Denial and defiance, 34–36,
    210, 215
Disappointment, 164
Disconnect, 1, 9–11
Distractions, 112
Doctor frame, 149–150
Dopamine, 14, 113–116, 194
Double-helix DNA structure, 95
Draper, Don *(Mad Men)*, 120
Due-diligence analyst, 121

Economic forces, 99–100
Emotional manipulation, 84
Emotions, 199
Empathy, 157
Enjoy your work, 92
Enterprise Partners, 168–169
Eradicating neediness, 157–170
    basic formula, 165
    beta trap, 162
    causes of neediness, 164–165
    disappointment, 164
    example (Enterprise Partners),
        168–169
    rules, 168
    self-protection, 160–161
    Tao of Steve, 166–167
    threat, 161
    time frame, 165
    weakness, 163
Example. *See* Case study (airport
    deal)

Eye contact, 162

Fear alarms, 14
Fisher, Ron, 158
Focus, 212
Four-frame hot cognition stack,
    135–137
Frame, 21, 24, 43, 208–209
Frame collision, 22
Frame control, 19–68, 209
    analyst frame, 44, 51,
        52, 60
    denial and defiance, 34–36
    example (avocado farmer's
        money), 41–48
    example (cop frame), 25–26
    example (money center bank),
        31–33
    frame collision, 22
    frame disruption, 33, 46
    game, as a, 211
    guiding principles, 24–25
    intrigue frame, 52–61
    intrigue story, 56–59, 61
    plowing, 45
    possible opening phrase, 67
    power frame, 30–36
    prize frame (prizing), 37–40,
        62–68
    rational arguments, 27
    social dynamics, 23
    time frame, 49–51
    what is it, 22
    who owns the frame, 49
Frame disruption, 33, 46
Frame master, 36
Frame stacking and hot cogni-
    tions, 129–156
    cold cognitions, 155

Frame stacking and hot (*Cont.*)
  decision making, 130–131,
    132, 147
  example (defaulted debt),
    133–136
  example (Helen Woodward
    Animal Shelter), 143–144
  example (Mother Teresa),
    150–152
  four-frame hot cognition stack,
    135–137
  hot cognitions, 130, 153, 155
  intrigue frame, 137–143
  moral authority frame,
    148–152
  prize frame, 143–146
  time frame, 146–148
  wanting, 136, 148
Framing, 3
French waiter, 71–76
Fundamental human behaviors, 64

Geyser Holdings, 6
Global status, 92–93
Goldhammer, 178–206
Goldman Sachs, 134
Golf pro and cardiac surgeon,
  84–85
Gordon, Evian, 107
Greenberg, Sam, 46, 172–183
Guiding principles, 213–216

Haynes, John-Dylan, 131
Heart of the pitch, 123
Hedge fund manager, 87–90
Heightened states of emotion,
  199
High-intensity push/pull pattern,
  119

High Tech Ventures (Bell), 124
Hookpoint, 5, 46, 90
Hot cognitions, 52, 130, 153,
    155. *See also* Frame stacking
    and hot cognitions
Human behaviors, 64
Humor, 35, 68, 210, 211, 214

Idea introduction pattern,
  105–108
Idle social banter, 92
Impression of someone, 98
Information gap, 116
Intrigue frame, 52–61, 137–143
Intrigue ping, 5
Intrigue story, 56–59, 61
Investors, 67

Jaws, 60
Jaywalking, 77, 86

Khosla, Vinod, 158
Kincaid, John, 135
King-of-the-world moment,
  169–170

Law of large numbers, 23
Lao-Tsu, 166
Light-heartedness, 210
Likeability, 136–137
Lingua franca, 217
Local star power, 33, 73, 86, 91
Lord, Jack, 167
Low-key, low-intensity push/pull
    pattern, 118

Mad Men, 120
Majors, Lee, 167
Man-in-the-jungle formula, 141

Martini making, 113
McGarrett, Steve *(Hawaii Five-O)*, 167
McGhan, Donald, 41–44, 48
McGhan, Jim, 44–48
McQueen, Steve, 166–167
MediCor, 41
Medium-intensity push/pull pattern, 119
Midbrain, 8
Momentum, 92
Money, 67
Money center bank, 31–33
Moore, Geoff, 105
Moral authority frame, 44, 45, 148–152
Mother Teresa, 150–152
Movement, 102–104
Mystery stories, 116

Narrative pattern (intrigue frame), 140–143
Narrative thinking mode, 139
Neediness. *See* Eradicating neediness
Neocortex, 8, 9, 111, 154, 210
Neurofinance, 5
Neuroscience, 8
Neurotransmitters, 107, 113
Nonreactive state, 53
Norepinephrine, 113, 114, 116
Novelty, 114–116

Obama, Barack, 149
Old-fashioned sales techniques, 152–153

Paradigmatic mode, 133
Pecking order, 70

Persistence, 158
Personal story, 55–56
Perspective, 21
Pitch techniques, 95–128
    attention getting, 112–116
    backstory of the idea, 100
    budget, 124, 125
    change blindness, 102–103
    competition, 125
    heart of the pitch, 123
    idea introduction pattern, 105–108
    movement, 102–104
    novelty, 114–116
    overview, 97
    phase 1 (introduce yourself/big idea), 97–109
    phase 2 (explain the budget/secret sauce), 109–127
    phase 3 (offer the deal), 127–128
    phase 4 (stack frames and hot cognitions). *See* Stack frames and hot cognitions
    push/pull, 118–120
    secret sauce, 125–127
    tension, 117–122
    three-market-forces pattern, 99–101
    time-constraint pattern, 96
    time constraints, 96, 97, 126–127
    "Why now?" frame, 99–105
Playfulness, 94
Plowing, 45
Point of view, 21
Porterville incident, 57–59

Power-busting frame, 28, 30
Power frame, 30–36, 211
Power frame collision, 33
Power frame disrupter, 33
Practice, 212
Prepitch thoughts, 190
Presenter's problem, 4
Presidential campaign
    (1984), 209
Primal lever, 54
Prize frame (prizing), 37–40,
    62–68, 143–146
Public spaces, 81
Push/pull, 118–120

Qualifying question, 94
Quantum Fund, 132

Rational arguments, 27
Rational decision making, 130,
    132, 133
Reagan, Ronald, 209
Real life example. *See* Case study
    (airport deal)
Reducing the autonomy of
    choice, 197
Rules of engagement, 14–16

Satisfaction (Berns), 114
Scarcity bias, 147
Scheiner, David, 149
Secret sauce, 125–127
Seinfeld, Jerry, 126–127
Seized status, 200
Self-protection, 160–161
"Selling," 153
Selling hard, 119
Simplicity, 110, 214
Situational status, 70, 85, 93

Six Million Dollar Man, 167
Smucker, Craig, 9
Social barriers, 78–82
Social dynamics, 23, 67, 210
Social encounters, 149
Social forces, 100
Social frame, 23
Social position. *See* Status
Social threat, 107–108
Soft touch, 214, 215
Soros, George, 131, 132, 155
Southwest Exchange, 42
Spielberg, Steven, 60
Spinach vs. chocolate, 153
Stacking frames. *See* Frame stack-
    ing and hot cognitions
Starting up, 213–216
Status, 69–94
    alpha, 77, 78
    "being nice," 69
    beta trap, 78–84
    charisma/ego, contrasted, 69
    example (French waiter),
        71–76
    example (golf pro and cardiac
        surgeon), 84–85
    example (hedge fund man-
        ager), 87–90
    example (Walmart),
        82–84
    fluidity, 85–86
    global, 92–93
    guiding principles, 92
    how it works, 91
    jaywalking, 77, 86
    local star power, 86
    situational, 70, 85, 93
    your turf vs. target's domain,
        86–87

Straight from the Gut (Welch), 131
Surprise, 57, 61

Tao of Steve, The, 166–167
Taoism, 166
Technical details, 52
Technical material, 55
Technology forces, 100
Tension, 61, 117–122
Terminology, 217
Theory of mind, 111
Threat, 12, 161
Three-market-forces pattern, 99–101, 192–193
Ticking time bomb, 141
Time, 67
Time-constraint pattern, 96
Time constraints, 96, 97, 126–127
Time frame, 49–51, 146–148
Time frame collision, 49

Time pressure, 147
Timeliness, 92
Trade shows, 82
Trendcasting, 99

U.S. Air Force Training Manual, 202

Validation-seeking behavior. *See* Eradicating neediness
Vocabulary, 217

Walmart, 82–84
Wanting, 136, 148
Wasting time, 98
Watson, James, 95
Weakness, 163
Welch, Jack, 130
"Why now?" frame, 99–105
Wolfe, Tom, 2

Zajonc, Robert, 145, 148

About the Author

Oren Klaff is director of Capital Markets for the investment bank Intersection Capital, where he raises tens of millions of dollars from investors and institutions. Intersection Capital has grown to $250 million of assets under management by using Klaff's pioneering approaches to raising capital and incorporating neuroscience into its capital markets programs. Klaff is a specialist in financial modeling and the codeveloper of Velocity, a capital markets product that has raised over $100 million of private equity and venture capital. He lives in Beverly Hills, California.